THE MINGUS PARCHMENT

The Secret to Becoming a Successful Entrepreneur

Walt Sutton

May this winter's tale of tumult and tomatoes lead you

to the secret of your own business.

CANDESCENCE MEDIA

www.CandescenceMedia.com
info@candescencemedia.com

Quantity sales. Special discounts available on quantity purchases by corporations, associations, and others. For details, contact the "Special Sales Department" at the address above.

The Mingus Parchment/ Walt Sutton. -- 1st ed.

Cover design and illustrations: Scott Berry
Interior design: Gayle Evers

ISBN 978-0-9900219-7-1

Not all who wander are lost.

J. R. R. Tolkien

DEDICATION

"Why did you become an entrepreneur?"

"I am just doing what I love," she answers.

"But why did you become an entrepreneur?"

"I don't consider myself an entrepreneur," she says.

"But listen, you have done it. You have this thriving little business. What was it that made you choose this path?"

"I am just doing what I am good at, what I love, nothing special."

She pauses for a moment then adds, "It's also a way to feed my family, you know?"

For twenty-two years I've been traveling the world asking successful entrepreneurs this one question. They almost always respond with bits and pieces of the same answer. These entrepreneurs are amazing people, but they don't consider themselves amazing or even noteworthy. Nor are they comfortable having someone like me turn a spotlight on them.

This book is dedicated to the whole tribe; the amazing, wildly diverse, eclectic, self-sufficient, clever and ever-so-hard-working entrepreneurs and would-be entrepreneurs of the world.

And in particular, *The Mingus Parchment* is dedicated to Jan King who, as an entrepreneur herself, worked tirelessly to keep this book alive. Jan is without doubt the all-powerful, enabling Goddess of Glimmerland. We in the Forest will always be grateful for her help and encouragement.

CONTENTS

INTRODUCTION

"Keep your eye on the meatball!" That's Mother's voice—in my head.

"I will," I say even though she is not in the room. Her voice is impatient-sounding, but I have to explain some things first, otherwise this story won't make sense and who wants to read a story that doesn't make sense?

"Just remember." Her voice again.

"I know, I know, Mother," I wave a fully loaded quill pen in the air. "See here? I am starting."

I live in a different land, one that is attached to but mostly separate from your part of this world. I live in a village, one of 137 villages loosely connected in a Forest confederation called Glimmerland, named for a famous war hero who saved this part of the world during the last invasion by the forces of evil. The Great Glimmer passed on seventy-six generations ago but we remember her and her valorous contribution to our people in many ways, including naming the largest of the dwarf confederations in her honor.

Dwarfs, you ask? Yes, you see we are a race of dwarfs, the

children of war and peace, peace and war. Our history is replete with battles, some disastrous, some victorious, all characterized by death and destruction, and all having left their mark on dwarfish society. The cycles of invasion and counter-invasion lasted longer than we dwarfs can remember. It was the Great Glimmer who changed the axis of destruction to an axis of cooperation. It should come as no surprise that our Forest, as well as numerous monuments, trails, and outcroppings, have been named in her honor.

Since her time, we have experienced steadily growing prosperity. Villages have developed into bustling towns, farms have grown to villages. Crops grow better when you don't uproot them and soak the ground with blood every five years. Farmers live to farm, milk, and collect honey. Our metalwork, millwork, leather-craft, food preparation, brewing, mining, homebuilding and every other important aspect of our economy is better than last year, which was better than the year before that—all the way back to the adoption of the Glimmer Codex, our governing document.

In Glimmerland, the prospects for a young dwarf couldn't be better. We educate our little ones carefully and safely through twenty years of required instruction. We believe in experiential learning, which is to learn "by hand." Our little ones learn and work their way through the curriculum, which admittedly takes more time then just learning each item "by head."

We believe that if you learn by hand, have a background of some head learning, and acquire lots of experience with which to guide your hands, you reach the one true learning: "doing learning."

After completing the basic curriculum, Glimmerland young'uns may choose one of several directions. Some opt to go right to work; others attend advanced hand school, where the basic crafts such as farming, brewing, construction, and many other skills are taught. A third alternative, taken by only about ten percent of the graduates, is to attend a dwarfish university, of which there are three in Glimmerland. There one learns to be a corporate leader, a head farmer, master brewer, leather conglomerate overseer, dwarfish philosopher, healer, parliamentarian, historian, master storyteller, or one of the many other professions.

That was another indirect legacy of the Glimmer Codex: corporations. Three generations after we achieved lasting peace and reliable prosperity, a rogue dwarf named Geekus bolted from our land to study at the Great Commerce Institute in the capital city, some eighty days' journey by cart to what seemed like the other side of the world. One of the learnings he brought back to our side of the earth was economy of scale; that is to say, big groups can do big things and big can sometimes be cheaper. Geekus wasn't universally appreciated for his social attitudes or behavior. His biographers all agree he was loud and opinionated. Nonetheless, much that he brought back to us has become part of our culture. Among his many ideas and innovations, none was more important to us than the corporation.

In the post-Geekus flurry of activity, we formed the Forest Exchange Commission to regulate and trade shares in corporations. We also modified our laws to make corporations legal and granted them the same status as individual dwarf citizens. What was once a quaint economy of small family businesses began forming and reforming into corporations of all sizes. Today there are thousands of corporations in Glimmerland, the largest seventeen of which make up the all-important Geekus index of shares, or the "Old Geek" as it's widely known. The "Old Geek" has been on a spectacular run, increasing in value year after year for over sixty generations.

What follows is my story, set against the background of our great Forest and the expanding economy of a developing dwarf nation. I have written it down because there is wonder in the economic world, and I hope you can benefit from it. But beware, because there is also great peril. Yes, my story is about business, in a way, but it's also about dragons, honey, magic, money, tomatoes, monks, and beer with all sorts of surprising twists, turns and curls. I lived this adventure, although that need not have been the case as I could have easily died once or twice along the way. In fact—well, you'll see soon enough!

1 ~ THE WAY OF YOUNG DWARFS

I am average height for a dwarf, just short of four feet tall. I, like others of my race, love color—lots of it—and we don't bother with matching or complementing. So our dress looks like a kaleidoscope of different-colored doublets, smocks, singlets, robes, capes, and boots. We wear stockings, not socks. We get around by walking or riding in wagons (two-wheeled and four-wheeled) pulled by donkeys—small donkeys by your standards.

My childhood was, as my parents will attest, a prodigious source of stories about the difficulties of raising young'uns — that's what we call all young dwarfs, young'uns. I was the one who accidentally lit our thatched roof while making a fire stick. I was the one who inflicted a nasty gash on my own ankle while playing with my father's sword. I was the one who was asked to leave storytelling class because my story had more to do with reproduction than the assigned subject—something about herbs, as I recall. My childhood was a trial for our whole family, my teen years a trial for our whole village, and my young adulthood has been a test for large parts of the Forest.

This has not been an intentional bout of destruction or insubordination, but as my mother (Wanda the Wishful) reminds me: "Pretty is as pretty does, and ugly is as ugly does." She is a wonderful dwarf mom, a hard working senior executive for an insurance company and a caring home person, but she is given to fits of doggerel, especially around me. I think they make her feel better, but they don't seem to have helped me much other than to populate my head with an overabundance of embarrassing bits of folk wisdom that I routinely choose to ignore.

My father (Wallace the Wise) is just as bewildered and frustrated as Mother, but he skips the quips and gets right to the head shaking.

They have been married forever, so I tend to get it from both sides. Mom will be spouting something like "A dolt and his gold are soon parted," while Dad, like a badly-rigged puppet, stands looking on, his head bobbing from side to side.

Dwarfs are big on education, so hand school and university are open to everyone, free of charge. My parents were pretty pushy about my going all the way through university. I graduated after six years (the courses are set to match your learning pace) with a degree in high dwarf corporate leadership, which is to say I could one day be eligible to become a middle manager in one of our mega-dwarf-corporations.

When I almost flunked out of dwarfish university it was Mom who saved me. She went right to the top and pled my case. Being a prominent person, her cause (the writer of this tale) was given yet another chance. I made good on it too and graduated, albeit last in my class. She then pulled strings and got me a job as trainee with her employer, one of the seventeen pillars of the Old Geek, the esteemed Bassenwaith Connistar Pty, Ltd.

She had plenty of cautionary poetry to prepare me for the big event. I was to start my career as a memo-sorting sub-clerk-trainee, lesser grade. They are very big on titles at Bassenwaith Connistar Pty, Ltd. As Mother observed, "They have a knack for putting folks in their place."

It was a yellow-and-green autumn morning when I marched away from home for my first day on the job, sporting the company junior-grade uniform of a red singlet with forest green trousers. This was it! I was heading in the direction marked "adulthood." My parents still talk about how much this day meant to them.

As Mom and Dad tell the story, they cried. I know I cried. I was walking away from them, so they couldn't see me, and that was good. After all, every boy and girl in our Forest goes through the same experience. I wanted them to see me composed and ready for the adventure—at least from behind.

Later that day a state contractor for moving young'uns' effects arrived at my parents' house and loaded the three trunks that held all my worldly stuff. My effects, as the manifest called them, were delivered to my new home: an apartment in Transition Meadows, a rent-subsidized project where most of the young'uns in our part of the Forest begin adult life.

Following the great conflict some sixty generations ago, the problem of grown children staying at home had developed to the point of a confederate-wide crisis. Prosperity was building, jobs were opening up, but kids refused to grow up and go out to work. They were avoiding growing up by simply living at home and financially shackling their families for decades. In the old days there were wars to fight, and children were sent into the army or supporting services, but without wars, kids just didn't seem to get it. Dwarfish society tolerated this until a survey showed that seventy-five percent of graduates were staying home, and most never went out to work. It wasn't good for society to have all of these adult children leeching off their parents and the community. Finally, a select subcommittee of bedraggled parents came up with the idea that all children had to grow up. It became a simple and universally accepted law: when you leave school, you leave home.

That day at the office, my first ever, I learned many lessons about work, especially about laboring at the bottom of the pile. I was the lowest of the low, my work was repetitive, and the criticism was pointed and severe. The more meager the task, the harsher the commentary. As it was explained to me, I was an apprentice spear-chucker in a hundred-tier army, the basement ant in a very tall anthill, the bottom bee in our elongated hive, an underlings' underling. And then there was the cheerful note about it taking six or seven years to advance to the next lowest level of Hand Work, one of many levels to be traversed before I might be considered for Head Work and a "thinking" job. Not that a thinking job was any kind of a certainty, just a remote possibility as long as I did a good job of not thinking for a long time.

2 ~ A PROMISING FUTURE

First my green pants were replaced by blue ones, then my singlet went from red to orange to puce then black. Those first three years on the job were a whirl of changing colors, each change announcing a promotion. I was a dwarf with a promising future! My pay was still meager, but it was 20 percent less meager than it had been when I started. In the euphoria of accomplishment, I was seriously considering a move from Transition Meadows to a real neighborhood, one befitting my promised status. Perhaps I should say potential promised status, because I was still mired in the least important stratum of a vertically overwhelming organization. My mother's position, for example, was listed six pages above mine—not that I would ever begrudge her the success—she has always worked harder than anyone I've known.

I began that fourth year at Bassenwaith Connistar Pty, Ltd in the copy-checking department as a delivery clerk. I was working for our broken window subsidiary. My job was to take the insurance policies as they were released by the mail room, put them in order by policy date, and deliver them to the copy clerk queue chief, whose job it was to coordinate the flow of policies through the giant copy department.

The hard part about my job was getting the order right, as there were many dates appearing on the face of each policy and those nimrods in the field never seemed to get the right date in the right square. I developed a bad attitude about our sales force, and worse, for the first time in my working life, I was assigned to a supervisor who was old, mean-spirited, short-tempered, and operating with what I suspected was a half basket of fruit.

Mingus Mulchwood was a lifer-loser. He had thirty-two years, six months, and three weeks' seniority. I know this because Mingus would greet each new employee in his charge with a sneering calculation. "Do you know when I began working here at Bassenwaith Connistar?" he would growl, as if it were a question. He would then nimbly subtract your starting date from his and announce the difference as if he hadn't figured it out in advance. Every new employee in the copy department was greeted this way, but I seemed to provoke something even darker in this angry old dwarf.

"Don't sneer at me you little undereducated upstart half-dwarf toadstool. Seniority is all that matters around here, and you will be following well behind me as long as you are in this organization!"

And that wasn't the worst of it.

The explosion of our economy and the subsequent development of certain large organizations bred a particularly virulent form of bureaucracy with all kinds of rules and rituals intended to keep people from getting out of line. A seniority system, a carefully disguised caste scheme, numerous power cliques, and rules about rules about rules characterized the working world of my era.

The most strictly enforced of these rules was that no dwarf could ever be promoted or moved from a department without a supervisor's positive recommendation. The idea here was to give the corporation strict control over employee movement within the organization. We are a society that values order, having fought so many wars. The spirit of this rule was honored not only within companies but also—as a courtesy—among companies as well. Since the Geekuses employed half of the people in Glimmerland, and since a large percentage of the other companies relied on a relationship with one or more of the Geekuses, the net effect was that this creep, Mingus Mulchwood, had complete power over me. He was both supervisor and jailer.

"I wasn't smirking, sir! It is an honor to work with a dwarf of such experience and distinction…sir!"

Buttering up this Mingus was hopeless, at least as far as my brand of butter went. He hated my guts, and there was no accounting for it. The second day he greeted me with: "You, dwarf, are the worst of a bad lot! I swear I'll make you into someone useful if it kills you!"

His glowering face became a regular feature in my workaday routine. I began to feel my promising future turn mushy, its potential rotting like a peach from the inside out.

I tried, really I did. In lockstep with our procedures, I would carefully gather the policies, sort them into issuing date order, and run to the copy desk which was a hundred yards from my sorting station. Pick up, sort, run and deliver, over and over, knowing that as soon as his face appeared—and it could appear at any moment—he'd catch some error, some bone-headed mistake I'd inadvertently made.

To this day, I don't know how he knew, but he did. His hand would grab my singlet and spin me around. Then he'd flip through my sorted stack. We'd lock eyes and his would wrinkle in a smile as he'd hoist the misplaced policy high above his large dwarf head, bellowing to everyone in the long hall, "Don't have to use the teaching manual in this group, do I? No sir, not as long as we are graced by the ineptness of this young idiot! Look! Another cock-up! Another prime example of what not to do! See this, everybody?"

My mother tried to be helpful. She didn't know Mingus, but she knew the type, she said. She recommended that I appeal to his fatherly side. We were having a family dinner celebrating the High-Monthly, a regular national holiday for family gatherings that falls on the twenty-second day of each month. On High-Monthly day, every family gathers for afternoon storytelling and dinner, followed by some drinking and a lot more storytelling. Graduated young'uns are allowed back home for the High-Monthly celebrations after a year's absence.

At this month's High-Monthly there were forty-six of us, all related in one way or another. The way we keep High-Monthlies interesting is to gather with different branches of the extended family, and this month we had joined with Mother's older brother and related kin. Now Mother, she's a prudent drinker, but her brother and related kin are ardent consumers of anything alcoholic. So for this High-Monthly we ordered double beer and several cases of mead, knowing we were all in for a real party. It was the mead that empowered me to approach Mother about "Mulchface," as I'd come to think of him.

"Now dear, every person has an unpleasant side. You've just got to figure a way around it, and I'm pretty sure calling him Mulchface behind his back won't help your attitude."

"No, Mother, but he screams at me, laughs at me, tells others I'm a nimrod—and most of the time it isn't my fault! None of my other supervisors were ever this mean!"

"No, I understand, a dwarf like that can be terribly difficult.

But I don't know of a single successful executive in any of the Geekuses who hasn't had to face the same sort of thing. There is no one single answer to this kind of conflict. You're just going to have to persevere until you see an opening, and my guess is that opening will have something to do with his warmer side."

"Mother, Mulchface is colder than snow iced over a frozen swamp. There *is* no warmer side!"

"The mead is making you stupid, my dear. Everyone has a warmer side."

And that was it. That was all she would tell me. When I started whining again she just held both hands in front of her as if to block my sniveling sounds and shook her head from side to side like Dad.

I took it for six months. For six months, I read dwarf-help books to buttress my plunging spirits. I drank more mead than was good for me. I visited a wizard and asked to have my defenses strengthened. I even started whistling while I worked. Eventually, even Mom became impatient and forbade me from talking about what she called my compatibility problem. "A grousing goose gets plucked first and is cooked for sure," she hissed at me when I broached the Mulchface dilemma.

I was stuck. Back and forth, sort and deliver, intercept, bark, hoist a mistake, and yell and scream and push me back into the routine. The more I worked, the more worried I was, the more errors I made, and the more often he did his victory dance. It was a sickening cycle, spiraling downward.

One day as I finished my midday meal I found myself in the cafeteria, frozen in my chair as if I'd been hit by a sudden devil-ray or paralysis. I hated the thought of going back to that office. And so I, like so many other workers in the world, discovered that I loved my time away from work ever so much more than my time at work. Thank the Gods, I didn't move up from Transition Meadows! Who knows how long I'd be able to hold on?

To compensate for a miserable work life, I took up Forest trekking and spent all my free time in the woods: walking, picking mushrooms, searching out fairies, listening to shushing streams, crunching through mountain snow, and breathing the clean, free air. I was becoming a bit of a Greenie (a naturalist, in dwarf jargon) and wished every day that I didn't have to go to work. But I did have to go to work. Part of the Glimmer Codex clearly stated that all dwarfs must earn a living; all dwarfs must work at least until they have enough to retire. I hardly had enough to subsist, let alone retire. I was at the beginning of life's cycle, not anywhere near the end. And that damn Mulchface was blocking the way!

Trekking helped some, but I was still tense. I added meditation, then acupuncture. Finally I said to hell with all of the fuzzy indirect stuff and started hitting the cheap wine bars around Transition Meadows, hitting them hard and often. I surrendered to an almost daily after-work pattern of dragging my frazzled and deflated dwarf self into the Grape Sucker's Cave and embracing serious chemical relief. And for three or four hours it worked well. The mornings were a little tough, but who cared? Mulchface was all that awaited me at the office, so a little extra pain didn't seem to matter. I even started fantasizing about Mulchface missing work because of illness, Mulchface being injured in an accident, and finally Mulchface's ashes in an urn, being lowered in at the company burytorium. I liked the last fantasy best, even though it made me feel like a wicked dwarf.

3 ~ THE LAW OF BEING, APPLIED

I didn't mean it, I really didn't mean it! Of course, frustration can lead to all sorts of excess, but there I was, arriving shakily at the office only to discover through a crashing headache that there was no Mingus Mulchwood waiting to pounce on me. To be honest, it didn't register properly for an hour, and what a blissful hour it was too. A full hour of collecting policies, sorting them, and running them to the copy desk, one time, another time, and yet another time without being accosted by the chief ogre. Finally, the unaccustomed joy in my work jarred my hung-over senses. Mingus was missing.

"Have you misplaced my august supervisor," I asked the woman in charge of "roll-taking and absentees."

"Why no," she blurted, "you haven't heard?"

"What?"

"He's sick."

"Oh, what is it—an advanced case of unpleasantness?"

"Perhaps." She clicked her gum while talking. "But I think it's the heart attack that's causing him the most trouble. He's real sick, I tell you. We sent the company doctor to his house to see if there was something we could do to help."

She paused for a fit of chewing, like an overly hungry squirrel. "When the doctor got there she carted him off to the hospital."

I was feeling sick to my stomach, thinking wildly, "I didn't mean it, really!"

"Are you gonna go see him?" she asked, smiling.

"Why would I want to go see him?"

"Out of respect, friendship, courtesy—you know."

"I don't think so. As it happens, we don't share any of those feelings for one another."

She snapped her gum with disapproval, but said nothing more.

"Is he going to live? I mean, is he dying or something?"

"Well." Staccato chewing. "Heart attacks aren't exactly like a hangnail you know."

"So I've heard."

The rest of the day was a blur of collect, sort, deliver, collect, sort, deliver, back and forth, swooping from one place in the office to the next, smiling much of the time. I was struck by the fact that this job, minus Mingus, was damn pleasant. Working without all that fear and ridicule gave me an almost giddy feeling of competence. Back and forth I walked, then ran some, back and forth, felt even better. Soon I was shuffling policies like a seasoned magician.

That night after work I stopped in as usual at the Grape

Sucker, had a quick blast of purple-pomegranate dwarf merlot, decided one was enough, and retired to my apartment to do some reading.

Relaxed and pleasantly fatigued, I settled in by a freshly laid fire. Breathing in the scent of burning peat, I quickly lost myself in a story of dwarf heroes from long ago.

The next day Mother and I were alone in the kitchen. A party of family and friends were outside under the canopy of trees, waiting for dessert. We were preparing trays of sweets and I was about to carry out the first of these, a couple of dozen honey bombs, when her hand gripped my shoulder and turned me towards her. Her blue eyes took me in, then narrowed.

"Are you going to go visit him?"

"Don't know why I should. He wouldn't visit me unless he thought it would make me sicker."

"You may be a little young to know that for sure."

"Yes, Mother, I am young, but I've got this one pegged. He wouldn't even consider coming to see me if I was sick, and I can't think of one reason in the world why I should act any differently towards him."

"I have no reason to doubt what you say. Yet there are times in life when good manners and the Law of Being take precedence over anything else, and dwarfs who've suffered heart attacks must be visited! You know the saying: 'What goes around comes around and around and around and around.'"

And so it was that on the following Saturday I made my way several miles across the Forest in search of Mingus's home. There were twenty or so single cottages scattered like leaves across the open space in the woods, each roof a different color ranging from red to dead brown. This collection of cottages was one of the new scatter-developments where the Forest and the houses coexisted in the same sort of randomness found in nature. The developer called it Spread Leaf. (Research has shown that developers in all societies tend to wax eloquent when naming their projects.)

I went from door to door, comparing the symbols with the address I'd looked up. Finally, there it was—three frogs and a willow bough: Mingus's address—as I'd copied it from the company register.

I stopped in front of the red door and wondered if I should knock or pull the bell cord. After this effort, I didn't want to scare him to death by pulling the bell, so I knocked lightly against the shining red gloss paint.

I knocked again, harder.

With a rush of Forest air, the door swung open. "Yes, yes, what is it? What are *you* doing here?"

Before me stood a bent old man wearing a rumpled blue bathrobe, with a gray, sleeping cone-hat pulled low over his forehead and ears. He'd lost none of his glower, which suggested that his meanness hadn't been affected by the heart attack. The whole specter startled me.

Most of us have had experiences with someone who gets our goat, a person who has a special hold over us, someone who makes us babble when we are otherwise coherent. I started to babble, and after an interlude of stuttering and hemming and hawing, he cut in.

"Well you clearly aren't going to be able to get it out stuck here on the stoop. Come in, if you must, and we'll get to the bottom of this."

A white, thin, shaking hand reached out from the arm of the bathrobe and tugged me across the threshold of Mulchwood's house.

4 ~ THE DWARF GETS A MESSAGE

I felt like a frightened child as he guided me through the gloom of a darkened hallway, past several closed doors, and into a cluttered, low-ceilinged chamber with just the spark of a fire remaining in the stone hearth. He pushed me into an old stuffed chair, and my head fell back against an antimacassar which may at one time have been white but now matched his gray complexion. I swallowed, and although the silence was uncomfortable, it was better than my babbling.

Mingus walked, hunched over, to the chair opposite the fireplace. He turned towards me then, and collapsed into the overstuffed seat with an old man's sigh.

"Come to bait me have you, come to see what the Gods have made me suffer? Well?"

I couldn't get any words out.

"Pleased to see me on my back? Why of course you are, why else would you come to this place. Or were you just passing by?" He laughed a dry, coppery laugh, then coughed and resettled in the chair. Blue-veined hands grabbed harder at the overstuffed armrests, as if to launch him to another attack. "Well? *What are you doing here?*"

He couldn't yell. He just hissed the words out past phlegm and spittle. Suddenly I imagined him dying right here in front of me. My punishment for wanting him dead would be to watch him choke and writhe and twitch and gasp to death. If I didn't say something soon that was exactly what was going to happen.

"Uh, well, my mother made me come to see you—oh, sorry—well…that's really it, she made me."

"Your mother? Your *mother*! What business is it of hers? What busybody thing is she up to?" His voice showed remarkable strength for someone about to die. "Afraid to come herself, is she? So she sends her little twerp out here to spy on me, to report back to them. Is that it? Your mother! Tell her to mind her own business!"

"No, I don't think it's that at all. She was worried about you, at least I think so, and she has a strong belief in community. She told me that a dwarf who's had a heart attack must be visited, and since you've had a heart attack and since I work for you, I was the one who should visit."

"Not believable! That is not believable! You must think I'm a nimrod! Not believable!" His face was flushed, and his sleeping hat fell off into his lap. He refused to let go of the armrests, as if he was gaining energy from the chair.

"Listen, I'll leave. I don't want you to get sicker. This was a bad idea. Mom just misjudged your dwarf nature, sorry to have bothered you!"

"Misjudged what? What is it she's trying to find out? Why don't those people leave me alone?"

"I don't know what you're talking about. Mom isn't one of 'those people.' She was just trying to do the right thing."

"Well, you little canker, how would you like to be dying, sick to the gills, and have everyone turning on you, everyone trying to kill you because a sick dwarf is an expensive dwarf, and expensive sick dwarfs can only get worse? Make no mistake—it's me alone against the people I've given my working life to. How would you like to be sitting in my old body today? Tell me that!"

"But my mother, she doesn't want you to die. She just thought I should visit."

"Yes, and twist the blade a little and get what's left of my heart tripping over itself. They tried to kill me with the company doctor, but I knew all about her. I threw her out, told her I wouldn't take any of her poison, so the company spy sends you, and the Gods know there is no one in the world that gets under my skin more than you do, better than poison by a long shot. You visit, I die, and it leaves no mark. You visit and report back to them, and they send you time after time until I give out and am off the medical dole, inanimate, dead, cold, buried, and decidedly inexpensive, terminally inexpensive!"

"No, my mother…"

"Your mother, the doctors, the personnel department, that woman in charge of absentees with her snapping gum and cheeky, disrespectful mouth, all of them are trying to kill me!"

Mingus pushed himself to his feet, raised his fist, and shouted (as best he could): "*Trying to kill me, but I won't let them! Go back and tell them you've failed!*"

He shook out his words and just hung there, looking at—no, through—me, past me, to some place on the other side of the room.

I got up and went over to him, helped him back into the chair, placed his hands in his lap and sat down on the floor in front of him. He was cold, and I wondered if someone could be living and dead at the same time.

"Don't worry about them, old man. You're going to kill yourself if you don't calm down. Be quiet a moment, and we'll just sit here awhile." I rested my hand on top of his, and we sat as the room darkened into late afternoon.

Mingus's was a musty old place, but neat. A faded, hooked rug covered much of the floor of wooden planks. Our two chairs, a small sofa, and a round, gnarled-wood coffee table were the only furniture. There were paintings on most of the walls, small oils, hard to see in the subdued light, pictures of flowers, fruit, and mountains. There was also a small, painted group picture— ten or so dwarfs gathered in a meadow in bright light. Mingus was sleeping, so I stood up to look closer. Carved on the bottom section of the frame were runes, dwarfish letters, spelling out The Joyful Family of Mulchwood.

"What are you doing over there? Get away from that picture, it's mine."

"I know it's yours, I was just looking."

"Why, why were you looking at that picture?"

"It's so joyful, like the inscription says."

"What do you know about joy? How can you even say the word, knowing you're here to murder me?"

"Look, I think you've lost your cork, old dwarf. I came here because my mother told me to come. She told me to come because she's an ethical, caring dwarf, and I've done what she asked. But she didn't say I had to come here and subject myself to your abuse. In fact, I've long ago had enough of your nasty tongue, your suspicious, unkind nature. I, sir, have had enough of you! Good luck with your heart, old dwarf, that is if there's any left!"

Reaching the front door, I jerked on the handle and let the late afternoon light flood into the hallway. I took in a big breath of cool forest air and went out, slamming the door behind.

A thrush twittered above. I set off down the path away from the house and watched a squirrel scratch its way straight up the side of an ancient oak tree. It was near the leaf season, and some of the oak was turning from green to yellow. A puff of breeze knocked several leaves from above and set them sailing through the air, falling all around me.

"Wait, you! Please wait!"

I didn't hear him, I was lost in the relief of being out of that house.

"Please, I am sorry, I am truly sorry. Please wait, please— you may be the only one who can help me!"

I stopped without looking back, breathing deep gulps of cold, wet air, not wanting to ruin this feeling of release by turning towards him, not even wanting to let his words into my head.

"I think I've made a mistake, please, come back just for a moment."

I'd never heard him say "please" before, not once. Nor could I have imagined this pleading tone coming from that caustic mouth.

"All right, what is it?" I was back in the house, feeling

claustrophobic again.

"Let's assume your story's true, that you're not one of them, that you're operating as a decent dwarf might. I've been on your back since the first moment you came into my department, I've been unfair and rude, pushing you all over the office, and yet you listen to your mother and come to visit me when I'm sick."

"Yes, it seems preposterous, doesn't it?"

"Yes indeed, but if you aren't another agent from Bassenwaith, then I may be in danger of making an even bigger mistake."

"Seems to me you've already made it—that you've enjoyed making it. I haven't had a good night's sleep since I started working for you. I've been driven bats trying to get your mean-spirited behavior out of my head. You got my goat, you old dwarf, and I think I hate you for it!"

"Yes, then perhaps I've made the mistake. No, I don't care what you think about me. For the most part, you're right, I am a difficult dwarf in the extreme. But I come from a family that knows something about joy. In fact, I was once joyful myself. Yet I, like the monsters of old, have metamorphosed from young and joyful to old, angry, and resentful because I made a fateful decision long, long before meeting you. I let that damn company squeeze most of life's joy out of me."

He paused for breath, wheezing through clenched teeth, before continuing. "I thought you were here to finish the job for them. But there is another way of looking at all of this if you'll just bear with me a little. In a matter of ten minutes or so we may both know something new and important about each other, and perhaps life as well."

5 ~ MINGUS IN ANOTHER LIGHT

"I was once a joyful young dwarf, not unlike yourself. We were a big family. I had ten brothers and sisters, all raised in a happy household on a farm near the northern mountains. I graduated high in my management class and began my new life at an older version of Transition Meadows."

Mingus was well settled in his chair again, the back rising high above the sleeping cap. He pulled and combed his beard with his left hand as he spoke.

"I was tagged as an up-and-coming Head Worker at Bassenwaith. I was full of myself and ready to do anything for advancement. I so wanted to be a Head Workers' Head Worker, a member of the Inner Upper Management Council. So when they said sort, I sorted perfectly. When they said copy, I copied with care and skill. I was an excellent company dwarf, often embarrassing other less-dedicated dwarfs in my work circle. When I saw dwarfs slacking, I turned them in. When I saw rules being broken, I called the offenders out. I was dead certain that the company appreciated my exceptional effort, and as if to prove the point, I moved through the bottom rungs of the endless ladder at a faster pace than most of those around me.

"In those days, Bassenwaith was in transition. They were

trying to make a move from the fifth to the second biggest company in the Forest Exchange. This meant "reinventing," at least that's how they put it, "reinvent." After ten years of moving up, often by sacrificing the reputations of fellow workers, I felt I was on the cusp of breaking through into Head Work. Then we were all told of the Great Push Upward, a day-to-day sort of surgery that was at the heart of this "reinventing." The Great Push Upward was aimed at eliminating inefficiencies and ultimately pushing (hence the title) Bassenwaith to number two. I literally dreamed of riding the wave of "reinvention" to the Inner Upper Management Council."

"But then something strange happened. Four of the dwarfs I'd ratted on were moved from Hand Work to Head Work. I was a little surprised, but thought of this as an oversight. A simple mistake made by an otherwise intelligent council. Then I discovered the mark! It seems that one of my newly promoted enemies put a mark on me. A black mark in my personnel file that would forever condemn me to be a Hand Worker."

Mingus stretched both arms upward, resettled himself, and continued.

"Outraged, and certain that my loyalty would be recognized, I decided to buck the system. I circumvented all channels, went over many important heads and approached a member of the council."

He smiled, one side of his mouth turned up and the other downward. "I carefully explained myself to her. All that I had done for the company, my willingness to report anyone who was slacking and breaking the rules, I told her all about it. I told her how several of these troublemakers had been mistakenly elevated to Head Work, and how they placed a black mark on my good name in retribution. I shared my deep fear of rule-breaking dwarfs being mistakenly promoted. I pledged my undying allegiance to the company, the Council, and the Great Push."

Mingus paused, folded his hands beneath his chin, sighed, and smiled.

"It took only a few seconds. Her mind was already made up. She explained it as if talking to a young'un. Simple, direct—that was her way. She said that she believed in team loyalty more than anything in the world. Her idea of integrity was to be true to your team members first and last. That was it. I was wrong then and wrong now, condemned to remain a Hand Worker for life. The mark was indelible. It would remain with me as long as I stayed with Bassenwaith Connistar Pty, Ltd, and I would toil in the bowels of the organization until retirement."

The old man shook his head slowly. "I was crushed. I lost every bit of optimism and energy I had about life and my work. They couldn't fire me, and since there are few places lower than sorting and copying, that was where I stayed."

"Why didn't you go somewhere else, old dwarf? Why not leave the company?

"Listen, you—I was scared. I had been unfairly marked, and who knows how far the influence had spread? I had a job, and I decided that no matter what they did to me I would pay them back by retiring out of the place. And that, come to think of it, is what I am about to do."

"Yeah, with a bad heart! What were you thinking? And by the way, when did you become such a jerk?" I quickly covered my mouth. I couldn't believe I'd said that!

"That's quite a question for someone so young...is there

more to it?"

I removed my hand, which was probably a mistake. "Seems to me that a person who's been through what you say you've been through would be more sympathetic to newbies like me…I mean, what's up with that?"

He paused, frowning. "Perhaps you weren't getting the right message."

"Right message? Right message! What other message is there other than you are, or at least were, a first-class jerk."

"Yes, true, a jerk and then some, but why do you think I was that way?"

"Huh?"

"Why do you think I acted like that? Did you like working for me? How long do you think you could have lasted?"

"I don't know, but what's that got to do with anything?"

"Well, since I was not ever going to promote you, eventually you would have gotten the message—the message being, my young dwarf, *get out of this company* before they do to you what they've done to me."

"But my mother, she doesn't think that—she loves Bassenwaith."

"She's been lucky, I think, and she has had a couple of guardian spirits—people she doesn't know about who have protected her from many of the bad actors in our organization. I don't think she really knows how bad it can be there, and remember, it's been years since she's been anywhere near the Hand Work part of the organization."

"So what are you saying—about me, I mean?"

"You, young dwarf, are a bright, promising person. When you came to my department I believed that the best I could do on your behalf was to blow you out of the organization and send you on a path with greater chances for fair treatment and a happy future."

"Why didn't you just take me aside and say so? Why did you make it so hard on me?"

"Because my experience is that young dwarfs don't listen to the advice of old dwarfs. Young dwarfs like to make decisions for themselves based on what they are experiencing. You get some grief and you get going. That's the sure way. I've been successful with twenty-nine others like you, so I've had some practice at this."

"And now you've had a heart attack. What's next?"

"Now I can be a very expensive retiree, that's what's next. You can rely on the fact that I will never appear in the sorting and copying department again, and I hope that the same holds true for you. I hope it very much."

"But what will I do?"

"Follow your own advice: look elsewhere."

"But what if all of the big companies are like Bassenwaith, or what if I run into another older dwarf like you, only this time he or she doesn't have my best interest at heart, what then?"

"Life is an adventure, isn't it?"

"Yes, but…"

"And you must embark on a new one soon."

31

"But I don't want to. I have a job, and they can't fire me. I can stay there forever."

"And make the same mistake I did? You're beginning to sound like me at another age."

"But I don't know what to do, and you're telling me I have to do it anyway. This is just a big mess!" I clenched my fists and shook my head in frustration.

"For now it is, but there are many options before you. Why not start there?"

"Fine for you to say. You stayed and held on and acted like a jerk. Why do I have to risk everything, break away and go out into the world?"

"Because you aren't a jerk. Because you have real joy in your life, and you can go outside without being marked as a bad dwarf. You could leave tomorrow with a good recommendation and prospects for the future—unless you would like to be sitting here thirty years from now, with a poorly spent life behind you and a broken heart?"

"That's no choice at all!"

6 ~ MINGUS FROM THE OTHER SIDE

There was no winning this argument. I felt trapped by his logic. I decided to busy myself at something else, something to break the tension, so I pulled together a meal for the two of us. It was pleasant, working alone in silence, listening to the birds chirp in the late dusk and watching the first flicker of fireflies appearing star-like in the meadow. The company nursing staff had delivered a small selection of food. The kitchen window was open, and a soft breeze brushed past me into the house and out the open front door. Soon the nights would turn cold. This airy reprieve was welcome.

I carefully placed plates of food, a pitcher of beer, and thick slices of crusty bread on the tray.

I stood there over the tray, staring, savoring the silence for a couple of minutes before bringing our evening meal into the living room and setting the feast on the coffee table between us.

Mingus looked at me, at the tray, and then back at me. "Well, there's something you hadn't thought of—you could be a food server!" His beard stretched sideways as he smiled, and he coughed out a chuckle.

"Thanks, I don't know why I didn't think of that hours

ago."

"Yes, well, you're just getting used to this newfound freedom. We must walk before we can run, young dwarf."

"You sound like my mother."

"Thank you, that's quite the compliment."

Large pewter spoons scraped against our plates as we doled out dinner, a meat stew with orange root vegetables in brown gravy. Say what you want about the company, they did send good food to their ailing Mingus, along with the corporate promise of delivered meals as long as he was sick. Mingus ate two bites, then settled back in his chair with a sigh. I was very hungry and cleaned my plate before eating several chunks of bread slathered with a soft yellow cheese. The beer didn't seem to appeal to Mingus, so I drank the entire pitcher myself. Assuming they weren't poisoning the food, Mingus was set for life. He was promised food, lots of beer, doctors and medical support, and a pension. The more beer I drank, the better the deal looked. I wondered if I shouldn't just say to hell with it and go back to sorting and copying.

Mingus began to snore, his beard buried in his chest. I ate until there was nothing left and settled onto the couch for a nap, dozing away to the sounds of his snoring and the silence of the Forest on a mild fall night.

I was walking through a low-hanging dark wood, feeling lost. The fear caused me to turn around, but as I started back, a bony, blue-veined hand reached out of the ground and started pulling me under, into the earth. As I was being pulled down, the dirt turned to gold coins. The blue hand was joined by several others, grabbing me, pulling me some place under the earth. Finally, the whole scene turned bright gold, and a dragon's head appeared in front of me, with smoke spewing from a crown on its huge head. The dragon opened its mouth, jaws agape. The smell of death blew over me in a hot, wet blast, and I started to scream.

I jumped up from the couch, in the dark, sweating. My mouth was dry—coated with the ripe aftertaste of hops. Mingus had moved his chair in front of the living room window and was staring out at the fireflies dancing all around the dark meadow under a moonless, starry sky. He was smoking a bent bone pipe carved in the shape of a dragon's head, smoke pulsing out between its singed white ears.

"Fitful dreams, young dwarf? You were yelping and twitching like a sleeping pup."

"Mingus, why should I trust you?"

"Because you know I'm telling you the truth. Of course, if you doubt me, if you really suspect I'm up to some sort of ruse, then you shouldn't do anything I say. In fact, if you believe I'm lying you should leave right now, don't you think?"

"Yes..."

"Well?"

"Damn, it's just that I don't know what to do."

"Well, to start with I've drafted a letter of commendation for you. It says that you are a good dwarf, and the work you did in my department was exemplary. I will get it sealed officially by the Dwarf Resources Department. With this letter, you are free to go where you choose. Why don't you sleep some on that, and we'll talk more tomorrow."

He limped into his sleeping chamber, and I heard his snore

begin as soon as the creaking bed frame announced his arrival.

I curled up on the couch, and we both slept well into a bright sunny morning.

We faced each other again over tea and bread at the dining room table. I felt better and more able to confide. "The immediate problem is that I have to work to live, and I also have to look for a new position at the same time."

I'd caught him with his mouth full, but he talked and chewed at the same time. "Indeed, but every return requires an investment. You'll have to work harder than normal to make this investment pay."

"Okay, so I make the investment, get a position with another of the Geekus giants and run into the same problem. What then?"

He was still chewing. "Perhaps there are other options?"

"Like what, be a food server?"

"Well, what if you worked for yourself, what about that?" He swallowed with a gulping sound and jutted out his lower lip, as he often did when challenging someone.

"You've got a lot of nerve! You live here, safe in a house paid for by Bassenwaith, and you suggest I risk everything to go out and become a merchant or a farmer or a self-employed trader?"

"Perhaps I'm suggesting it because the price of this house was too high, because if I were asked to pay it again, I wouldn't. You're quick to judge, mostly because you're afraid."

"I don't even know where to start with all of this."

He looked at me, pulled his lips in tight, and cocked his head a little to the side. "Well, you could start by asking for help."

My stomach hurt. I had a headache. I felt helpless. I took a sip of tea laced with honey. I waited him out. He just sat there looking at me. I waited longer, until, with a sigh, I relented and asked him for help.

He sat up straight, full of some invisible energy. The color in his face rose from gray to pink as he ran to collect parchment and pens for both of us.

Reseated across from me, he was animated, smiling, breathing fully. "Here we go, young dwarf. Here we go, we'll start at the beginning!"

We spent the rest of the day talking about who I was, what I could do, and who I knew. We made lists of skills, weaknesses, friends, and enemies, and we imagined all kinds of small businesses that I might like to start or run. As the possibilities grew, as I recognized those things that were bad for me, checked off those things that I was good at, and thought of all the people I knew who were in fact small merchants, I felt more and more energy until it became almost impossible to sit still.

Hours later, we had finally drafted a plan. I would go and talk to people who could give me information about different types of businesses. I would spend a month collecting real dwarf-data and would return to discuss my findings with Mingus.

We worked together through another dinner, more stew, and lots more beer—for me—and again I slept on his couch. The following morning I was due back at work. I left in the predawn gray, groggy and wishing I could quit the stodgy old company immediately. But I was a well-bred dwarf, and Mother's words—"Every dwarf must work for a living"—followed me off to Bassenwaith Connistar Pty, Ltd for yet another day of collect, sort, and deliver, collect, sort, and deliver.

7 ~ THE PLAN

I was never very good at independent research, so executing this plan was difficult from the start. Mingus, on the other hand, was a planning machine—methodical down to his bones. There were three main parts to the plan. First, I had to discover facts about the Hand Work parts of the other Geekus corporations, assemble them, and learn what I could about working for another large company. Second, I needed to see if there were any opportunities in farming. One thing I learned while working at Mingus's house was that I don't like sitting still—the more activity the better—so a life as a business owner, a mover and a shaker, sounded good. Farmers fit that description well, with the benefit of adding physical labor to the mix. Lastly, I needed to locate some small business owners. I would go to the source, small business owners or small business runners, and learn what I could about their careers.

Plan in hand, I worked by day and gathered data by night and on weekends. The farming and small business tasks led me back home. Father was raised on a farm. I also remembered that two of the extended branches of his family were liberally populated with small business owners.

But first I had to come clean with my parents, tell them

what had happened with Mingus and what I was trying to do.

It wasn't easy, what with Mother being a high Head Worker executive with Bassenwaith Connistar Pty, Ltd and Father—well, Father is very conservative and rather quiet. He too is a Head Worker, but for a small banking firm, and he has never quite approved of the entrepreneurial sector of our economy. I told them about the visit and my plan, then waited for the bomb to drop. Father shook his head wordlessly. But instead of the disapproving frown I'd expected, the ends of his mouth were turned upward.

"An undercooked rutabaga is hard at the center, so be careful where you bite or a tooth may be your price," Mom recited. "Are you sure you're ready for this type of adventure? Seems to me you've had very little experience at this sort of undertaking. In fact, it seems like you've had very little experience period."

"Mother…"

"True, Wanda," my father quietly agreed, "but we both know he must find his own way in life, and his plan isn't suicidal or even irresponsible. That's a big step for this young dwarf, don't you think?"

"Of course, Wallace, but there is so much he could learn at Bassenwaith, sheltered from dangers he knows nothing about. Perhaps in a decade or so…"

"Wanda, in a decade our young one will be another Mingus. That's what I am hearing. And another Mingus is not a happy outcome for anyone. You've prospered there, but our young dwarf, for whatever reason, has been created with a streak of adventure, and this sounds like a great adventure responsibly undertaken—thanks to Mingus. After all, our young dwarf is still working. If the perils of being a farmer or a business owner or a business runner are too great or dangerous, then our young dwarf can transfer to another Geekus company and continue life as a corporate person."

"That's right, Mother, really. I don't know if I want to go out and start a small company. I really don't. The best answer may be another Geekus, but one with a different attitude. Mingus has given me this wonderful recommendation, so I'm free to move as a good employee. But first I want to find out about all the options, and you could both help me a lot!"

Mother rested her chin on her small dwarfish hand, elbow propped up beside her still-full plate. I looked into her warm blue eyes, as I had all throughout my life.

"How can we help, son?" Father smiled and nodded.

I asked her to invite the small-business branches of our family to the next High-Monthly and asked if she would help question some of the family members, because I couldn't possibly get around to all of them in one evening. She agreed.

Later, I set about interviewing Father about life on a farm. We spent the rest of the evening together while he told me stories about himself, his family, his grandparents, and what it was like to be a farmer. As he told it, farm life was direct, hard, uncertain, and central to the dwarf he had grown up to be. He explained that his choice to go into banking had been a reaction to the farm, and one he'd never regretted. Our conversation lasted three hours during which we shared more than we ever had as parent and child. At the end, he reached out and put his hand on my shoulder, saying he needed to go see his father and have the same sort of conversation. We sat like this for a long moment, then we uncharacteristically hugged and I left. It was well after midnight.

8 ~ CUP HALF-FULL (OF DATA)

I was trotting, which is not my normal dwarfish gait. I'm normally a saunterer, a dwarf of slow sliding steps. But this morning—Saturday, a week after our entrepreneurial High-Monthly—well, I couldn't keep my feet under control, trotting and skipping all the way out to Spread Leaf and a meeting with Mingus.

Mother and Father had proved great interviewers, and my relatives had been remarkably forthcoming—as long as we kept pouring the wine and beer. The prize was a load-full of advice and data about the life and tasks of those who start businesses, those who run them, and those who own them. Our first important discovery was the name. Apparently the word entrepreneur was too finicky, too ostentatious for dwarfs who start businesses. So entrepreneur dwarfs typically used a simple contraction to identify themselves. They called themselves Dents, as in Dwarf Entrepreneurs. Dent, a good solid dwarfish sounding word—one syllable that said it all as in "Hello, I am a Dent, what do you do for a living?"

Pouring over the material was like drinking from a fire hose. Dents, as it turns out, have remarkably diverse and chaotic experiences, and yet Mingus had made it clear, "Don't come out here blabbering like some idiot, dumping all sorts of unexamined, random material on my table. You must gather, process, test, parse, and reassemble the information." So I'd rushed home each night, passing up the wine bars in favor of my second job: thrashing through the Dent interviews.

Friday night, after leaving the office I burst into his living room, startling the old man awake. He hadn't been asleep long because his pipe was still smoking, but he still jumped. "Good Gods! Young dwarf, my heart, remember!"

"Sorry, Mingus, I'm just excited. I've done what you said. I'm done with the work, and I'm ready. It's so exciting!"

"Yes." His chair creaked as he shifted forward to retrieve his pipe and knocked it on the ashtray until the moist plug surrendered its hold and fell out, smoldering. He then began the loading and packing ritual, his eyes never leaving mine."Yes," he said, "Go on!"

Now Mingus was an orderly dwarf, a dwarf who had become increasingly intolerant of chaos and loose thinking. He was one of those dwarfs who was fiercely concerned with how something is presented, impatient with what he described as "flapping around like a fish on the floor." I didn't want to jeopardize my findings by letting nervousness give way to flapping. Clearing my throat, I gathered my dwarfish thoughts and began the session by summarizing the conversations with my mother and father. I told him about the High-Monthly guest list, naming off the Dents and describing their companies. I reminded him that some of the Dents were owners, some were hired presidents, and some of them were Dent wannabees. I then summarized the data, reading from a list I had prepared on a piece of parchment. It read like this:

The Dents Parchment

- Most Dents love what they do.

- Most Dents don't want to do anything else.

- Most Dents find the job hard, scary, and at times lonely.

- Most Dents didn't start out wanting to be the boss.

- Many Dents say they could never work for anyone else again.

- Most Dents look forward to a different life after doing this job for some time.

- Many Dents want to change their part of the world, to set something right.

- All Dents want to earn some money.

- None of the Dents could tell me how they learned how to do this job.

The old dwarf's eyes squinted at the parchment I'd placed in front of him. His left eye drooped and teared up as he looked over my work. He wiped his eye with a red handkerchief.

"So what does this tell you about how to become a Dent, young dwarf?"

"Well...I should want to do it, and it may be scary and at times lonely, and I'm sick of my boss..."

"I can read, young dwarf! Address my *question*, if you please."

"I don't know. I learned a lot, but I don't think I learned

45

that. Come to think of it, I'm not so sure they know how they became Dents either. Perhaps it's an inclination, something they do because it's in their bones, or..."

"Data? Proof?" he broke in. "Points supporting your assertion? Do you have any factual observations for this notion?"

He shifted in the chair and looked harder at me. He stared and stared, and I began to shrink. I could feel myself getting smaller and smaller. "No, I don't have any supporting data except that we interviewed many successful Dents, and none of them were able to tell us exactly how they did their Dent work."

His gaze turned downward toward the pipe in his hand. The charred white dragon smoldered as he brought it to his lips and sucked. His head almost disappeared in an explosion of smoke. With Mingus, it was impossible to tell if he was in pain or thinking or angry, as effort and upset seemed to affect his face and body the same way. I thought I had failed, and felt a rising certainty that he was angry. I could imagine him abandoning me in the middle of this task, leaving nothing but a foolish young dwarf.

"Interesting, very interesting," was all he said for an interminable time.

"Hmm." He chomped harder on his pipe, old teeth clicking against the stem, and more minutes passed. I was too afraid to move and sat with my hands sweating as he chewed, grunted, and shifted from one elbow to the other and back again.

"Dwarf!" he shouted, and I jumped.

"Dwarf!" he shouted again. "You may actually be on to something!"

I was on my feet, heart racing, hands twisting one another

like cloth, still suspecting that any second he would pull the rug out from under my bare feet.

"Yes…Mingus, um, what exactly might I be on to?"

"Why they don't know how they learned it, that's what! Wake up, young dwarf, you have done very well indeed. The Dents, they don't know how they learned it."

"Oh!" I felt a stone forming in the bottom my stomach, a gnawing ache of uncertainty. I began to wonder if Mingus had suffered a stroke during his pipe-chewing deliberation. His ramblings reminded me of several fish flapping at the same time, bouncing around on the hard wooden floor of my imagination.

"Sir, Mingus, um, are you okay? I mean you're not supposed to get too excited. I'm sure you will be able to explain this to me, but for now why don't you just relax. I know, I'll make us some tea."

"Don't you 'tea' me, young dwarf! You must never patronize your elders! You have stumbled upon something very important, whether you have the wits to see it or not. Now get us some beer, a full pitcher and two cups. Tea, indeed!"

9 ~ IGNORANCE IS BLISS

"So," he began, after taking a sip of beer, "let's formulate. What is it you discovered?" He wiped foam from his lips and looked hard at me, waiting.

I drank two mouthfuls, thinking perhaps a looser brain would find the answer more easily. This was borderline torture. All of the data and my working papers were piled before Mingus like fallen leaves, worthless. He had just dusted them aside and was waiting for me to say something more, something I didn't know how to say. It made me angry.

"Look, Mingus, sir, if you have some brainy answer, why not just spit it out! I've told you everything I can think of, so it's your turn."

"Perhaps, but first think back and repeat what you told me right there at the end."

"What?" I barked. "That I failed, that I learned nothing in all of my work, that I don't have a clue about how the Dents do their work. I am *sorry* Mingus! I am sorry for *failing*."

"Stop, stop before you pop your dwarfish cork. Just stop! Calm yourself, have a little more beer. Now then, understand that I am quite pleased with the work you have done, only you need to work a little harder."

As I was about to jump up in protest he extended both hands, palms down, as if to smooth the space between us. "Calm down, relax, breathe a little."

I heaved in a roomful of air and emptied my chest one, two, and three times. I drank again, and leaned back in my chair.

"Okay. What now?"

"I want you to review your conclusions again, then repeat for me the conclusion that comes after not being able to find out how the Dents do what they do."

"Well, I just concluded, I just wondered, if the Dents know how they learned how to do their jobs, you know, in their own heads. I mean, I know they know how to do their jobs, only they don't really seem to know how they learned to be Dents."

"*Yes!* Stop right there! Sit back again, take another drink. You may relax now and bask in the warmth of dwarf genius, for that observation, young dwarf, is our much-needed breakthrough."

"Oh, well, thank you."

I was still wondering about the possibility of a stroke, but Mingus just smiled, no more questions, no poking or prodding. I watched him for another minute to see if this might be some sort of trick. He drank more beer, smiled again, and continued smoking his pipe. He even chuckled at one point. I certainly wasn't going to break his reverie and in fact would have been happy to sit like this for the remainder of the night. I had had enough.

"There, feel better?" he finally asked.

"Yes, thank you." I couldn't help myself—self-control isn't one of my long suits—so I went on. "I still don't know what the big deal is, Mingus. So what if they don't know how they learned their jobs, so what?"

"Well, here is so what. You gathered a blizzard of data from a lavishly loquacious gaggle of highly qualified Dents. You and your parents faithfully withstood the storm of stories, tales, anecdotes, and exaggeration. You faithfully recorded your data, sifted it, and reached many interesting conclusions about Dent life. Did I forget to compliment you on your collection of conclusions? Hmm, I'm afraid I did. Congratulations on your collection of conclusions."

"Thank you."

"You're welcome." He smiled and seemed very satisfied with himself. "You did good work uncovering all of those conclusions about Dents, excellent work. But the conclusions you deduced won't help you reach your goal. They only describe outcomes of doing Dent work. They tell you nothing about really doing it. It's a little like discovering the winner's name at a chess match—good to know, perhaps, but completely useless if you want to know something about playing chess!" He stopped, smiling again, nodding at me as if to ask my consent.

I sighed and feigned a smile. The lump in my stomach was growing with each impenetrable sentence. I wasn't sure I wanted to hear any more.

"You might ask: Was this absence of information the product of intentional secrecy? Was it the result of a concerted effort at concealing the Dent methods of learning?" Again he paused, looked at me, cocked his head and waited.

I was frozen, the lump now pushing up into my chest.

His face spread, wide and pink, as he smiled. "Unlikely, don't you think? Very, very unlikely. These people, Dents, certainly share one trait top to bottom. They love to talk about themselves and what they do. What do you think the odds are that they were engaged in a conspiracy to conceal this information and, if such were the case, that all of them could keep their mouths shut for an entire evening?"

"Pretty small, I guess."

"The odds are infinitesimally small. Smaller than a dwarf at a giant's party. Smaller than a fleck of sand beneath the greatest mountain. The odds might even be zero. This can mean only one thing. These Dents don't have a clue as to how they learned to do their work. And there, uncovered before us, is your challenge. To solve the dilemma you must discover what they don't know about what they know."

"Huh?"

"You must learn how they learn, even though they don't know themselves."

"How?" Bile was burning in my chest and throat.

"I don't know, but together we can find out—assuming you're still willing?"

"Yes, of course, but don't you think there might be a more direct way?"

He smiled again, a genuine, old dwarf's, brown-toothed smile. "Well, there might be an easier way, only I don't have an inkling of what that might be, do you?"

The acid taste spread through my mouth. I swallowed the rest of the beer in my cup, swirling it around in an effort to kill the unpleasant taste. I gulped and belched. "Oops, excuse me. No, I don't. I guess we'll do it your way."

"No, young dwarf. This is not my way. We are going to have to do it the only way it can be done, knowing that perchance it can't be done. You may work and work at this and still not get it. What I am sure of, however, is that this is the path you must take."

10 ~ A BLAST FROM THE PAST

Mingus rose, went to the gnarlwood hutch beneath the window and returned to the table with the *Dwarf Book of Guidance*, a thick, gilt-edged, leather-bound collection of wise sayings from our multi-volume history, *Dwarfdom*. He slid his finger into the center of the book where the sacred sayings are listed. I am not a religious dwarf—although religion is an important part of dwarf culture—but when Mingus pulled the book open with equal pages falling to each side, I knew where he was looking. All dwarfs know something about the *Dwarf Book of Guidance*. Starting in the early grades, we learn a selection of the most important sayings and the stories behind them. In the last year of formal education we are required to take the standard course of dwarf ethics, which is really nothing but the application of much of the book's contents.

Metaphysics in dwarf culture deals with two hemispheres, the physical and the non-physical (sometimes called the mystical). Within this system, those dwarfs who are able to stay closest to the line between the physical and the mystical are considered advanced spirits. Thus the *Dwarf Book of Guidance* is organized into three sections of sayings. The first section deals purely with the physical world, the last section only with the mystical, and the center, sacred section, deals with those expressions having influence in both realms.

Mingus's stubby finger rested in the very center of the book, right where the most sacred of the sacred sayings are located. He exhaled slowly. "Hmm, just as I thought."

"Mingus, are you a holy dwarf?"

"No, but the sayings have often helped me, so I thought I'd take a look, just on a hunch. This sort of coincidence may convert me someday though." He shook his head and looked up at me, leaving his finger pointing halfway down the open page.

"The book suggests a way forward, young dwarf."

I've always been uncomfortable with hyper-religious dwarfs, and although I'd done the obligatory study—and even owned a copy of the *Dwarf Book of Guidance* (we were all given one upon graduation)—the idea of consulting the book as some sort of oracle rubbed me the wrong way.

"Mingus, I don't like superstition. Could we talk about this first?"

"You know what the book says, young dwarf?" He didn't seem to have heard me.

"No," I shot back.

"The book says: 'Life is curly.'"

"How nice, Mingus. Just what exactly do you think that means?"

"You are young, so perhaps this truth has not revealed itself to you through experience yet, but it is true, young dwarf, deeply true. You see, ever since Geekus and the reform of our economy, dwarfs have placed an inappropriate reliance on a linear relationship between life elements. Most of us have been seduced by empirical thinking. Most of us believe that we can always count on point A leading to point B leading to point C and so on. But life never really operates like that. Hence the wisdom, 'Life is curly.'"

"Oh, uh-huh. So?"

"So, we learn from the sacred center in the *Dwarf Book of Guidance*. We are directed to remember that real life twists and winds, often turning in on itself, which is what I think we are seeing here. Life turning in on itself. And if we are to figure out something about life, we must turn with it."

"Yeah, but what does that mean, turning in on itself?"

"I think it means that we must re-turn, or go back a little, in order to make some sense out of all that has happened."

"I thought we were trying to move forward, though, not back." I was feeling irritated by this twisting and turning riddle.

"I can see you're restless, but I think this is right, that we have to go back to the last place we were given a clue."

"Uh-huh, but what clue, and where was that?"

"The last place—the High-Monthly, of course."

"But we can't go back, it's over."

"Yes, but the Dents still exist, I dare say, and their love for food and drink remains, don't you think?"

"Well, yes, so what?"

"So, we must reconvene them, feed and water them, and ask different questions—observe them in a different way."

"Another party?"

"Yes, a Dent party. We'll pretend that we are celebrating their Dent accomplishments. I've never met a Dent who wasn't pleased at being recognized for his or her accomplishments, so that's what we must do."

"But Mingus, we can't re-invite them, it's against High-Monthly etiquette, no family group is to be favored over others, they will have to wait their turn."

"I'm not thinking of High-Monthly, I'm talking about a party, simple as that. Let's see, we could hold it at the Drink and Tell. An upscale storytellers' tavern would be the perfect place for what we have to do."

"The Drink and Tell? Mingus, I can't afford to feed and water all of those Dents at a place like that, what are you thinking?"

"I'm thinking that I will invest in you and your research. You will pay me back some day when you've started your business and can afford to retire your debt. Until then, consider me your first shareholder."

I was stunned. I shook my head, not sure what I'd heard.

"Mingus, I don't think…I appreciate your help, but I'm not asking you for money. I don't think I can accept your offer."

"Listen to me, young dwarf. I'm willing to back you based on the real expectation that you will pay me back. I believe it to be a good investment. If I didn't think this was worthwhile, I certainly wouldn't do it—do you understand me? Most certainly I wouldn't. Besides, it may surprise you to hear that I am learning along with you. I mean, it has been ten years since I've even opened the *Dwarf Book of Guidance*. I am quite enjoying this adventure. No, I am pleased to be your first shareholder. Now, let's prepare for a great party."

11 ~ AN UNABASHED BASH

The Drink and Tell, what a perfect place! It was new, hip with lots of action, great local brews, storytellers from all over—in sum, it was the hottest drinking and eating place in the Forest. Mingus had chosen the one establishment every Dent would want to visit, especially if someone else was picking up the tab.

Ah yes, the tab, there was a mighty blow. Hundreds for a night's free eating, drinking, storytelling, and listening. Hundreds I would have never guessed Mingus could afford.

We had asked the wrong questions at the High-Monthly, thinking that life was linear as opposed to being curly. The types of queries we made prescribed the answers, and as such the answers were of little use.

Mingus surveyed his long life and remembered that real learning comes from undirected conversation, and most often from stories. The problem was figuring out how to recognize and collect great stories while having a party. The two of us thought about the puzzle separately. I was imagining a vacuum hose attached to each Dent head, sucking out story after story. Mingus, on the other hand, decided that our best chance was to hold a contest. We would offer prizes to Dents who told the best stories. The proviso was that the story had to be about being a

Dent. That was Mingus's stroke of genius, for dwarfs—and Dent dwarfs in particular—love a contest, as we tend to be naturally feisty and competitive people.

We devised four categories for contestants. There were stories about starting out as a Dent; there were stories about failing or making big mistakes; stories about big successes as a Dent; and lastly, stories about ending the Dent career and moving on. With Mother and Father's help we would split the group into four tables. Each table with its own judge and a scribe to record the tales.

The doors opened at sundown on a Friday night, and we distributed gallons of beer to wave after wave of arriving guests. The club provided a master storyteller to act as master of ceremonies and coordinate the evening.

"Dwarfs, dwarfs, may I have your attention please! Dwarfs, we are thrrrilllled to have you all here at this great Dent storytelling gathering!!!"

The room filled with cheers. Cups were raised, and beer was spilled in reply. The master storyteller, standing on a table, raised both hands to quiet the crowd. "We are offering the greatest eating and drinking bargain of the millennium! You, Dent dwarfs, are encouraged to eat and drink as much as you like all night long!" The room erupted again in cheers and screams of approval. "In exchange we ask only that you enter one or more of our storytelling contests, located in the four corners of the room." More cheers. "The contests are open to all of you, and you may enter as many as you like. Winners of each contest will receive an all-expenses-paid vacation to the Sandy Sea and the Emerald Resort Center." The cheers deafening, and the master had to hold his hands high for over a minute while the overwrought Dents reacted to the free beer, free food, contests, and big prizes. "Now here is the catch: you must contribute at least one story and receive your telling button to be eligible for the prizes, so get on with it, and enjoy your night!"

There was a four-way stampede as Dents broke from the center of the room towards tables set up in the four corners of the room The stories rolled out from Dents of all shapes and sizes, men and women, old and young. More stories than we expected were told, some funny, many sad, some frightening, all of them full of the grit of experience. The scribes scribbled, eyes moving from storyteller to parchment and from quill to inkwell in a frantic dance, with no time to eat or drink. One young female scribe was sweating, and she held her head off to the side of the parchment so as not to wet her words as she recorded what she heard.

At midnight, the master storyteller climbed up on a table in the center of the room and rang a large hand bell, signaling the end of the contest. "Dents, young and old, Dents, may I please have your attention!" Although gifted with a powerful voice, the master storyteller had to repeat this call for attention four times, punctuated each time by the clanging of the bell. Finally the room was quiet enough to announce that the contest was over, and that the judges were tallying the scores. The winners and prizes would be announced in fifteen minutes.

By two in the morning everyone had left, the room was empty except for the cleaning crew preparing for the next day's opening. We sat together, exhausted. In the center of the table was a stack of parchment. Mother smiled at me, her bloodshot eyes proudly assessing the gold we had harvested: great Dent stories, almost a gross of them.

"Well, we did it," she marveled. "We got more than I would have believed possible. Oh how those Dent dwarfs love to talk!

Now it's up to you, Mingus, you and our young'un here to figure out what you've extracted. I do hope it leads to something more important to Dents as well, something many Dent-minded dwarfs can use. Wouldn't it be wonderful if you could figure out how they learn and what they learn? That would be very special indeed." She reached across the table and patted Mingus's gnarled hand twice, then took Father's, gesturing that it was time for them to leave.

"Thank you for your help, Mother, Father. This was quite a night, I think." My brain was seizing up from fatigue and overstimulation. I was one very tired dwarf.

12 ~ THE SEARCH BEGINS IN EARNEST

We awarded all four vacations that night, selecting a winner in each category. The grand prize went to the best of the best, Ethring of Eton's story. His tale about founding the Eton Honey Cartage and Ferry Companies was a story above stories. It was a story about starting out. Honey was at the heart of it, honey in the right place at the right time. It wasn't that Ethring was a great performer. His tale about starting out as a Dent was delivered in a somber, old-voiced monologue, for Ethring was a very old dwarf. The drama was intensified by the fact that his story reached back into a time unknown by most of those present, a time when young country dwarfs were left to develop more or less on their own. In his part of the woods, almost all young'uns either became farmers or were drafted into the growing nine-to-six legion of physical workers. The Forest-wide education system hadn't reached out into the country. So Ethring's story was doubly valuable because it described a time and place mostly lost two generations ago.

As a young dwarf, Ethring earned spending money by harvesting the family beehives. There were five of them in an unused pasture dotted with wildflowers, next to the Eton cottage. Standing barely knee-high to his dad, the young Ethring would take several hours to do this simple job. His small, uncoordinated hands would scrape hives and drip the nectar into clay mugs. Mother Eton would top the mugs with freshly melted wax, sealing the contents for delivery.

That was the dicey part, delivery. Although the Etons were working folk, earning most of their income from real nine-to-six jobs, the honey, a valuable commodity in the Forest then and now, supplied a delightful supplement for vacations, gifts, and cottage extras. "Honeymoney" was the frosting on the family financial cake, and times without honey were far worse than times with it.

If it were left to the bees, there would have been only times with honey, but making honey is just the first step in turning it into money. Ethring's father would take the sealed pots to a village broker who would write out a note of promise. According to the note, the Etons would receive 75 percent of the value received for honey delivered to the capital city, less one pot of honey for handling. When old Ethring told the story he paused here to explain the complex nature of the promises. "First, that the honey be delivered to the city and second, that we had to give one full honey pot and twenty-five percent of the sales price for this broker's service."

As Ethring put it, "Father might never have objected, except that many of our shipments allegedly never made it to the city. Furthermore, my parents made our own honey jars. Mother painted a green tree on the side of each one. Once, after losing three shipments of honey in a row, my father decided to investigate and endured the four-day trek from our farm to the capital. As he told us, those city folk were as thick as thieves, and he couldn't get them to admit that the honey had made it to market. But he did see several of our honey jars being used to dispense honey at a restaurant near the honey merchant's warehouse. There was naught for it but to believe that we were being bamboozled." At this point, the recorder reported, Ethring looked around the table at each of the listeners.

"Cheating happens," he continued, "and my father understood personal responsibility. He decided that he would figure out a way to get the honey to market and sell it himself. The thing was, we lived four days away from the city, mainly because the River Mead cut us off from the city's part of the world. It took two days walking upriver to reach the Mead Bridge, then two more days to get to the city. Honeymoney or not, Father couldn't afford eight days off work, so he designed wooden outriggers which he attached to our wagon to enable him to cross the river near our house. He told us that using this ferry wagon would allow him to reach the city and return in two days. I was still young, but I helped him find the wood and cut the lashings for the honey wagon and raft contraption. Because it was my father, I didn't think of questioning his scheme or the design.

"When we were done, he loaded the contraption with honey jars and headed to the Mead, a couple of hours walk from our farm. He pushed off into the dark blue course, proudly poling his vessel out halfway across the river. Then a wave hit and pushed one of the pontoons into the flood. Water rushed over Father's ankles into the wagon, knocking jars loose and sending them out into the river. In the next instant, my father fell sideways into the current, arms windmilling, hands reaching, and the raft stopped its passage across the river altogether. The flooded contraption slid sideways as it began to drift downriver, swamped and empty.

"Father, like so many of his generation, couldn't swim.

"I was to spend several years trying to figure out what happened, what it was about the craft that was flawed. I was also

67

trying to figure out how our family, without one of its two breadwinners, could bring in the money we needed to live. I was fixated on figuring how to get the honey to market safely. And so, fueled by sadness at my father's death, I built dozens of model boat-like devices and tested them along the river's banks. It took me a couple of years to come up with a promising design, and yet another year to build the test model. It was a scale model, about one-tenth in size. I tested it along the shoreline, filling it with river rocks to simulate the weight of myself and the honey cargo.

"Five years to the day of my father's death I set out from the shore, poling myself across the River Mead. I made the trip in about half an hour and fell on the bank in tears, holding the raft against the shore. I was glad to be alone so no one could see me, for in those days it wasn't appropriate for dwarfs to cry openly—even young'uns. As it turned out, that first crossing was the real beginning of the Eton Honey Cartage and Ferry Companies. All of what followed is rooted in Father's death. I had learned the most important lesson of all—survival. The sight of him toppling into the river passes before my eyes at least once a day. It is as if Father won't ever let me forget. My aim is to teach this lesson to my children too, only in a less-dramatic fashion, mind you. If the truth be known, however, I doubt they will ever appreciate life as completely as I do."

I was sitting with Mingus at his dining table, reading the record aloud. I looked over at him, wondering whether the best stories had anything to do with the best information. He was drumming his fingers on the waxed wood tabletop, breathing in and out with a smoker's growl. As I was about to speak he cleared his throat. "Survival, what do you think about that young dwarf?"

"I think it's a sad story."

"Yes, indeed, but that's not what I asked. What do you think the lesson is? Remember that we are trying to learn something about Dents, now."

"I think it's a very sad story, and he is still haunted by it."

"Indeed, but don't you think he learned something from it?"

"Well of course, but it wasn't worth it, not by a long shot!"

"Perhaps, but you've overlooked something rather important. Ethring had no control over his father's behavior. All he could do was watch. Many would watch and be so devastated that they would forget to learn. Ethring watched, suffered, and learned. Ethring's father taught his son that above all, you must survive."

"Yes."

"I think this is an important Dent lesson, don't you?"

"Yes," I repeated, too sad to say anything else.

13 ~ LOGIC AND ASHES

Mingus wrote the word *survive* on a blank sheet of parchment which he pinned to the dining room wall. "There. We are on our way. Survival is one of the experiences Dents must learn about because surely they must survive, as must their businesses."

The Mingus Parchment

• *Survive*

I was too upset over Ethring's loss to say anything.

"I think, however, that future lessons may be a bit harder to uncover."

It was a question of discovering something you didn't understand. Stories are helpful, we knew that, but neither of us had a clue about what a Dent's life was really like. I wanted to be one but had no experience. For his part, Mingus had lived life as a company dwarf from start to heart attack. We were going to have to move beyond the stroke of luck in deciphering Ethring's story and its message about survival. I found myself hoping that we weren't going to have to live through too much more sadness.

We tried several ways of looking at the data. One was to put all of the stories in chronological order. I had it in my mind that this might uncover some hidden relationship between the tales, but nothing opened up. In fact, this trick only seemed to add confusion to an already befuddled problem. We separated the stories into male and female stories, which was interesting but not particularly instructive as to how Dents learn and what they learn. We sorted them by industry, which was creative but, again, confusing.

"I wonder if we haven't incurred a great expense only to learn the simple lesson of survival," I complained.

"Perhaps, but we've just started, young dwarf. I think you are too impatient by more than half."

"Easy for you to say. Your best days have passed!" I flushed, hot coals surfacing in my cheeks as I heard myself. "I'm sorry…"

"Point taken," he sighed. "You are even more impatient than I thought. Well, fine, as you suggest, if I'd had some of your hot headedness as a younger dwarf, perhaps my early years would have been more rewarding. But here we are, two generations apart, and I'm not quite finished with living yet. Although I accept your inference about my life as a nine-to-sixer, I take exception to the suggestion that life is over for me. I am working to make up for the past with the present, and since you are the primary benefactor I would appreciate a little consideration for my effort." He paused for several seconds, looking at me, then added, "And for my considerable experience."

"Yes, of course, I'm so sorry. I don't understand myself half the time."

Mingus and I had been working all afternoon, and this being the cold time of the year in the Forest, night slammed down early around us. I lit a second candle and could see my reflection in the black window behind Mingus, my young face next to the shadow of his old body.

As if not hearing my apology he sat up straight in his chair, scratched the tip of his nose with a gnarled thumb, and spoke. "I remember a philosopher dwarf telling a class of bright-eyed and impatient students about the search for truth. We were second-year university dwarfs with unbounded confidence, the likes of which only lack of experience can produce. We were studying the issues of Place and Truth. After having debated several different methods of uncovering the truth about a theoretical place, we were using an imaginary village as the focus of our work. This old professor suggested the wildest solution I had ever heard. Wild, but memorable."

"Here is what the old philosopher told us. He said the best way to conjure up the truth about a place is to take the names of all of the people who live in that place and take all of the stories written about those people in that place and take all of the pictures painted and drawn of the people and all the stories written about the place itself—take all of these ingredients and make a great mound of paper and canvas. To get the truth you must then light the mound on fire and sit beneath a tree, some distance from the conflagration, in the path of the billowing smoke. As the smoke moves around you, you must put quill to parchment and begin to write. The truth about a place will be revealed in your writing."

"I hope you're kidding, Mingus!" His philosophical gobbledygook irritated me so much that I was tempted to just leave and go home. "We're rather heavily invested in these stories. I don't think burning them makes a lot of sense!"

"Yes, don't be so testy, young dwarf. A little imagination and a sense of humor are valuable traveling companions."

"You're beginning to sound like my mother," I growled.

"As usual, I take that as a compliment. Speaking of your mother, what does she have to say about this exercise?"

"Oh, she preaches patience even more emphatically than you, saying things like 'A stitch in time saves a bunch,' and 'Good bread rises at its own rate.' For all that, I don't like the idea of burning the stories."

"No, but the idea of resisting the constraints of logic has more merit than your age may, thus far, have allowed you to understand. Here's what I suggest: We shall end our evening tonight by reading all of the stories out loud. I will read one, then you will read one. We will do this until we have read them all aloud twice. Then we will quit for tonight and begin work the day after tomorrow, at dinnertime."

"What does this have to do with burning, Mingus?" I asked, shaking my head with impatience.

"We shall see, won't we, young dwarf, we shall see."

14 ~ ASHES TO ANSWERS

That night I slept the sleep of the dead, exhausted by trying to tug answers from pages piled high with stories. Since Mingus had insisted that the stories be left untouched for a couple of days, I treated myself with a visit to a small drinking parlor near my apartment. I needed to unwind, and did so by tasting a complete rack of foreign brews, trying one after the other in a grand international imbibing tour. Arriving home late, I fell into bed stuffed with brew and pub food. My sleep was fitful, painted with dreams of dwarfs, gryphons, and the full pantheon of Forest dangers. I awoke queasy and dyspeptic.

Work was a suitable punishment for my excess, and I suffered well into the late afternoon. Upon leaving the office, having duplicated and delivered remarkably few policies, I arrived at my apartment exhausted and unsettled. That night I slept the sleep of the sleep-deprived: deep, dreaming, and uninterrupted. I traveled with caricatures of the Dents who were a part of my new life, and we went on several adventures together. I dreamt of a great bazaar with rugs, honey, wheat, potatoes of all colors, carrots, baked bread, and several kinds of sausage I seemed to be hungry for. Finally, just before waking, I dreamt of a raft floating down the River Mead, without passengers or a pilot. It was just floating with a single candle lit in the center. Somehow the raft stayed in the center of the river. I followed it for what seemed like days until I finally woke.

That evening I hurried along the path from the office to Mingus's house. As I arrived, the food wagon was pulling away from his front door. I ran to help Mingus put away his weekly supply of food, beer, and wine. I was excited to get back to work. After a hurried greeting, I dispatched several boxes from the front step to the cupboard and larder considerably faster than I had duplicated and delivered policies for my employer. Mingus watched me as he drank his evening beer and smoked his pipe. The white dragon gurgled, and a cloud lingered around his head.

"Well, thank you, sir," he said mockingly, "your industry and consideration are noted and appreciated."

"You're welcome. I appreciate your appreciation," I mocked in return. "Only I must admit, I want to get to work, and I couldn't stand waiting until you were done with the unloading."

"Well, I'll have to be more careful to schedule our appointments around the food wagon then. This is a real bonus!"

"That's okay, as long as we can get to work."

Mingus pushed out his lower lip beneath the dragon pipe stem and squinted. His eyes signaled a smile. "Hmm," is all he said.

"I think I get the smoke now, or at least part of it—you know, the story about place and truth."

He said nothing, just puffed and sat.

"I've been dreaming about so many things the last two nights. I can't remember all of them, but one had to do with a huge bazaar, a limitless bazaar in which every imaginable item on earth was for sale. Many of the Dents we've met were there in the stalls, only this place was much bigger than our village market. It extended from me to the horizon. Each time I bought something from one of the Dents, he or she would smile and lift a little off the ground as if some magician had granted the power of levitation. If, on the other hand, I refused to buy something the Dent would slump, and shrink, and literally become shorter. I bought so much of a certain sausage that the Dent was flying when I left. I would buy a length, and he would smile and fly to the back of his booth, pass into the dark covered area where the supplies were kept, and reappear with more delicious-smelling sausage. The dream was so real I could smell the sweet blast of herbs that accompanied him as he levitated from the back to the front. Next, I dreamt about a raft drifting down the River Mead with only a candle aboard." I told Mingus about the sad feelings I'd had while accompanying the raft on its long, winding trip.

"Yes, and then?" Mingus puffed.

"That's it: the smoke, my dreams, the stories, all of the words floating around with the memories of the Dents. I was dreaming part of our answer, only I haven't figured out what the part is. Can you?"

"I don't know, tell me more."

"There were more booths and wagons than could be counted. People were running goods from somewhere out in the country into the booths, supplying them, while thousands of shopping dwarfs were going from booth to booth making Dents levitate or get smaller. I was only one in an army of shoppers. Uncharacteristically, too, I was only buying what I wanted. If a booth sold something I didn't want, no matter how persuasive the Dent was, I said 'no' and moved on. I was surprised at this, because I love to buy stuff and hate disappointing anyone, especially someone who is trying hard to sell something. I've often thought how good it is that I don't have a large income. I'm so weak that my apartment would be stuffed to the rafters with useless purchases."

Mingus settled his chin in his hand and considered. Only his eyes moved from time to time, up towards the ceiling, somewhere to my left, behind me, making contact with mine, then high up again. "Well," he began, "I hear you describing something with three elements. First there is selling versus not selling, which inflates or deflates the Dent. As you go about shopping in your dream, you seem to be afflicted by the characteristics of real consumers in a real market. In other words you will only buy what you want and nothing else. Thus, you go from stall to stall inflating or deflating Dents according to your wants, something the market does quite ruthlessly, I'd suggest. Secondly, I see something about the Dents getting goods into the stall to sell. Seems a Dent would be chronically deflated if the stall were empty of goods or if the goods were of such poor quality as to never sell. Lastly, the consequence: too much deflation, or an inability to get goods to sell, gives rise to the riderless raft, as it were, a floating icon of Dent death."

"Yes, that's right, Mingus, that's right! I remember now. In the dream, as supplies were brought from the country to the booths, Dents would argue about the price and shape and color and quantity of the goods. They were acting in an opposite humor to when they were selling to the shoppers, and I remember wondering at the transformation! You've done it, only…"

"Only what?"

"Well, I'm not sure what it means for me yet."

"Deals, dwarf, that's what it means, deals!" He sprung up from his chair without so much as a groan and charged to the wall and the parchment. Carrying it to the dining table, he rummaged for his quill and inkwell. His wrinkled old hands smoothed the parchment as he dipped the pen into the black pool, shook a drop from its point, then scratched *deals* underneath the word *survive*. He then made it into a sentence, "Make the deals."

The Mingus Parchment

- *Survive*

- *Make the Deals*

"Don't you see, you clever dwarf—no deals, no business, no Dent. That's how it works. The Dent must make or buy the products to sell, must have a place to sell them, must pay the taxes, must pay shareholders, must have relationships with all sorts of entities, just to get goods into the stall. Then the Dent must get customers to buy the goods. In short, the Dent must make a series of deals to survive; that's what you've discovered. And the price for letting too many of the deals go sour is a Dent's death. Deals! Dwarf, you've conjured an important aspect of Dent success by dreaming of making the deals."

"But it's just a dream, Mingus, I'm not sure I see what you are getting at…deals, I mean."

"Well then, consider our party at the Drink and Tell. Why do you think it is a popular tavern?"

"Because they have good drink and good storytellers."

He pumped the hand holding the dragon pipe for emphasis.

"Yes. That's right, and more, much, much more. As you suggest, there is the purchase of the correct drink for the right price, and the arrangements with the storytellers, again at the right price. Sure, those are some of the deals that have to be in place to create a popular tavern."

I was imagining the Drink and Tell Dent negotiating her beer purchases in a warehouse filled with kegs and cobwebs when Mingus interrupted. "And then there is the deal for the building they are in, and the deal with the decorators who made it look like an ancient hall with all the coats of arms and weapons. There are the deals with the staff who dress up in costume and serve the customers, the deals with the moneylenders who finance the whole thing, with the advertisers who got the word out, and with the customers. Good food, good drink, great stories, fun place—guaranteed. All of those deals and more must be in place to make the business work properly, and it is the Dent who must see to it."

"But Mingus, that Dent doesn't do any of those things, at least as far as I can tell. I rarely see her at the tavern and I've never seen her deliver food or drink, or tell stories!"

"No, nor have I. Good point. So there is something more here. The Dent doesn't have to make all of the deals. The Dent's responsibility is to see that the correct deals are made…that's it! Others can do the work, but the Dent is responsible for seeing the correct deals are made, with the proper terms and conditions. Good thinking, young dwarf. That's an important refinement, because I happen to know that she is thinking of opening a chain of Drink and Tells, and this higher relationship to deals is the only way such an endeavor could come about. Even a Dent is restricted to being in one place at a time."

Mingus chuckled and clanged his pipe against the thick

glass ashtray, emptying the ashes onto a smoldering mound of burned tobacco. Setting the pipe down, he returned to the wall and rehung the parchment. "It's time for some of that food we've unloaded. All of this talk about food and drink has made me peckish."

"How much more do we have to learn about the Dent life before I can seek my fortune?"

Mingus was already carrying cheese, bread, and a pitcher of beer to the table. He set his load in the center and returned to the kitchen for more. After three such trips we had a feast of fruit, bread, meat pies, carrots, beer, butter, and roasted hen. The orange cheese was pungent and spread easily on the thick-crusted baker's bread. I was beginning to wonder if he'd heard my question when he hummed a *hmm*, which was a reliable sign of something to come.

"Well," he began around a mouthful, "seems you can start whenever you want."

My heart jumped. I was ready to get out of the grind and go out and start a real business where people work hard and the rules are fair. "Because," he continued, "as far as I can tell from reading our stories, that's what most of these Dents did. They just went out and did it without knowing what the 'it' was."

"Oh," I said, knowing that there was more.

"But if you really want to know what Dents do, before you go out there, I think we have more work to do."

Just the thought of going out there armed only with a child's understanding of survival and deals had given me a chill. I was grateful for Mingus's admonition.

15 ~ WINTERGLOW:
A GOOD TIME TO THINK

Winter is a dark time of the year, festivals notwithstanding. The leaves are long gone, a memory of summer past, clothes are worn in layers against the cold, and the wind is so relentless it oscillates between blustery and blasting. Sunlight, the precious source of brightness and warmth, appears later and later each morning and departs earlier and earlier each afternoon, until one grapples with a fear that someday there might be no sunlight at all. Daylight is so sparse that we use a different name for the brief span of diffused gray light we get each day—winterglow. Any dwarf will tell you that winterglow is at best a euphemism for candle glow, which is the real light source of this season.

Our great storytelling party had been held in the fall, just as the leaves were turning, in the still-warm memory of a soft Forest summer. Anyone over the age of five knows what happens after fall, and since there is so little to do outdoors until spring comes around, I resolved to make use of winterglow to solve the Dent mystery once and for all.

I decided that, come spring, I would be starting my life as a Dent, brimming with the knowledge of successful Dents and budding like everything else that grows in the world. This feeling of being off on my adventure powered me through night after night of talking, sifting, sorting, imagining, and even recounting dreams. Life at Bassenwaith Connistar Pty, Ltd clicked forward in its boring, relentless monotony. A kinder old woman had replaced Mingus as area supervisor, yet between the winter and the drudgery, there was plenty of motivation to get my research done, so I forged ahead even though I didn't know what "done" would look like when or if it arrived.

"Have you given the old brigadier's story any more thought?" Mingus asked one night. We had read through a stack of "Leaving the Company" stories yet again. Mingus was fascinated by the story told by a retired army officer, Roger of Ragmut, Brigadier (Ret) First Fierce Forest-Thumpers. The main part of his tale had to do with turning over the reigns of his company to a successor and how difficult it was for him. Mingus, however, was more interested in the preamble to his retirement woes, the story's prelude. He told me to find the parchment and read it aloud.

In his army days, Roger of Ragmut, Brigadier (Ret) had led several hundred Forest-thumping dwarfs in the famous Thumper Corps. Theirs were dangerous and demanding missions. The thumpers would move forward of the standing army, pounding the ground with oversized wooden cudgels in order to attract enemy attention while the main forces maneuvered and shifted to gain the best tactical advantage. Once the enemy was attracted, the thumpers would, on command, scatter and regroup in another position and begin the ominous thumping again. The brigadier had seen many dwarfs die in defense of country. He was given to telling tales from the wealth of stories he had heard and lived, stories about honor, valor, and thumping bravery that most dwarfs would find implausible.

As a byproduct of his army career, the brigadier had a

heightened appreciation of the value of peace and order and, in particular, for the system of government, economic freedom, and justice as it existed in Glimmerland. Upon retirement, he settled onto a small country holding outside of Glimmer's second-largest village. He spent two years assembling his papers, writing his memoirs, and contemplating how he could best use the rest of his life to contribute to the society he held so dear. The answer was made plain to him one day in the midst of trying to get some manuscript papers from his farm to a publisher on the other side of the Forest.

As the story was recorded, Roger had explained: "Oh, the Royal Glimmerland mail is first-rate, certainly, but there are times when you just have to positively, absolutely, get a package from here to there by a certain time. In those instances, our postal system has nothing to offer. I lived my life understanding the meaning of timing, organization, efficiency, and dealing with the unknown, so it seemed that this undertaking was a perfect fit. I would start a rush delivery service, imbue it with the values and ideals that have been so important to me, and set a positive example for the greater society. We would employ people and create a wonderful service, all for the betterment of Glimmerland. And I would have done something worthwhile with the mature years of my life, as well as justifying my army retirement pay, by making this investment in our great place on earth."

Mingus, who was scribbling notes, broke in, "And of course he didn't just hire a bunch of ragamuffins with shoulder bags. He started a service of young, well-groomed, carefully trained courier zealots—or at least that's what they became as the result of working for him. At the outset he established standards for behavior and performance, hiring mostly for personality and attitude. He invested in each new hire by putting them through a three-month training program—three months, just to deliver a package!"

I, of course, had never been in the armed services, but the whole thing sounded a lot like the army to me. "Training like…boot camp, you mean?"

"Yes, I suppose it was," said Mingus, chuckling, "But isn't it interesting that today his training program is considered a jewel on anyone's resume? I can recall a number of Dents telling me that they sought out dwarfs who'd been through Thumper Express training because graduates were bound to succeed."

"Well," I said, feeling a rising sense of disdain, "Do you think it's the training or just the people they chose? You know— you get gung-ho type dwarfs and you beat the competition almost every time?"

Mingus was quiet for a minute. "What does it matter? It probably has something to do with both selection and training and the rules and the uniforms and the procedures and everything else that goes into working there."

"All right." I was still feeling defensive. I never was attracted to the chop-chop-spit-and-polish types, "So he made a little Thumper Corps, only this time for profit. What of it?"

"What of it?' Mingus repeated. "What of it? Well what about something like two hundred offices Forest-wide, the ability to get a package to the Gryphon Caves on the other side of the world in under eighteen hours absolutely positively on time? Or what about all those seemingly happy dwarfs running around in shorts with their shirts tucked in and hats alike and in place, being cheerful, helpful, and on time, and contributing an important service to our society? What about the fact that each of those dwarfs, wherever you encounter them, knows what to do and how to do it no matter what the courier challenge? What of that?"

"Yeah," I said, begrudgingly. "Maybe it's a little bigger than the Thumper Corps. Even so, I don't like those types of organizations."

"I see that, young dwarf, but that may not be the important point." Mingus was happy now, looking at me hard and smiling. He held this pose for a long moment, then raised his hand, thumb extended over his shoulder, gesturing at the wall behind him and the parchment.

"Have we learned something for the list?" I asked.

"Perhaps."

"Do you know what it is?"

"Perhaps."

Mingus's cheeks were red and the smile broadened. He let his arm drop, folded both hands on the table before him, and said nothing more.

"Mingus!"

"Yes, young dwarf!"

"Mingus, what's the answer, what is it we have to add?"

"Think of what the brigadier has done."

"Created a little army? Delivered millions of packages? Made a bunch of rules? Trained a lot of dwarfs? Bought a lot of uniforms? Learned how to select gung-ho dwarfs?"

"Yes, these are all parts of what he has done, but in a greater sense what has he done?"

"Made a big army? Like that?"

"And how could he have possibly done that if the people who worked for him didn't want to be a part of what he was creating?"

"What do you mean?"

"Well he has the rules, the uniforms, the boot camp, and now a history of millions of successful deliveries. He has values and ideals, and it would seem to me that if his employees didn't share some of them with him, there would be no Thumper Express. My guess, young dwarf, is that most of these people share the brigadier's values by having been attracted to them for some reason and then having had positive experiences as the result of working there."

Then it hit me. This was not just a little Thumper Corps! "You mean that he's made up a whole...society!"

"Yes!"

I was flooded with admiration for the brigadier. Disdain was replaced with a sea of appreciation for what it must have taken to do what he did.

Mingus rose, fetched the parchment and added the words *create a society* to the list. We agreed that through sheer force of will the brigadier decided what sort of company he wanted to run, what he thought was fair and unfair, and what his ethics demanded of himself and his employees. He'd then set out to create a society based on his findings.

"So writing his memoirs was an integral part of getting ready for the next step in life!"

"Yes," said Mingus as he rocked the blotter back and forth

over the newly added words. "And once he was clear about what he expected out of his society, he was smart enough to refine the model. After all, he was working with civilian dwarfs as opposed to army types. But it's quite clear throughout, he never relinquished his basic ideals. The society created by Roger of Ragmut Brigadier (Ret) is a model much envied throughout Glimmerland. And he built it, his way, from the ground up. What I think this tells us is that Dents are society builders. And within their business, they are the primary societal model or influence. If I were about to start a business, I certainly would want to know about this responsibility, wouldn't you, young dwarf?"

The Mingus Parchment

- *Survive*

- *Make the Deals*

- *Create a Society*

16 ~ MONEY IN AND MONEY OUT AND EVERYTHING IN-BETWEEN

Several days later, on a cold, washed-out Saturday afternoon, I sat in Mingus's living room complaining about the wet, the wind, the dank, dreary winter, and my salary. Clearly, becoming a Dent was going to take a lot longer than I had hoped. In the meantime I was asking him what he thought my chances were of getting a raise to ease the cash flow of being a young'un with expanding young dwarf needs. He wasn't very optimistic. The policies for raises at Bassenwaith Connistar Pty, Ltd were as rigid as one would expect for a place full of lifer-losers. Worse, the topic of money led to a more serious problem. Mingus had inadvertently discovered something I'd completely overlooked.

"You will need some capital to get going, no matter what type of business you start. Additionally, my guess is that you will also need access to some credit as you grow and develop your new company."

"Yes, well, what are moneylenders for anyhow?"

Mingus's head jerked. He looked hard at me. "Moneylenders? Banks? Well yes, they do lend money, but not to people like you, I'm afraid."

"What do you mean? Why wouldn't a bank loan me the money I need?"

Mingus barked out a laugh, which trailed into a deep chuckle. "Why in Glimmer's name would they ever want to do that?"

"Because I'll have a great idea, and they'll want to earn the interest from my business."

"Well, I certainly hate to be the voice of darkness, but you overestimate your attractiveness to moneylenders, for sure. Yes, moneylenders thrive on interest, but they only earn interest if the debtor can pay back both interest and principal."

Sometimes Mingus and his lately discovered sense of humor got under my skin. His quips and gibes drawn from years of life experience did, from time to time, make me feel like he was making fun of my youth and inexperience. "So what does that matter? A good idea is a good idea, and I'll find one!"

He rested his bearded chin on his folded hands and smiled. "I have no doubt you will come up with a good idea, young dwarf. But I daresay having a good idea is a long way from being a good candidate for credit or a loan."

"Lots of the Dents we talked to borrowed money, lots of them!" My voice was loud and cracked as I strained to make my point.

"Yes." It seemed that the smiling would never stop. He just grinned out his words. "But what they may not have mentioned was the not-so-trivial matter of collateral."

My upset was spilling over. I could hardly stand listening to him anymore. So, perceptively, Mingus stopped our session and simply gave me an assignment. "This week, young dwarf, I want you to go and talk to your own selection of Dents. Pick several whose stories are convincing, dwarfs who strike you as being credible. Ask them about borrowing money. When you've done that we can continue our conversation."

"But I know I'm right about this, I want to talk about this now!" The smile finally abated some and Mingus cocked his head sideways, old piercing eyes burrowing in. "Go do your work. If you are right, as you so strongly feel, then you will still be right after you do your homework!"

What a week! It was one rude awakening after another. I left the cottage intent on proving the old man wrong only to discover that he was righter than right, that he spoke with a voice of reality, and that my squeaky dwarf's musings were fantastic, silly, and incredibly naive.

I did six interviews in all, supplemented by an embarrassing conversation with my parents. Truth be known, I wish I'd just talked to them first, for the relationship between borrowed money and interest and repayment of loans is known to most adult dwarfs.

All of the Dents I talked to said borrowing is a big part of the game, although the extent to which each used indebtedness varied. One younger, beginning Dent said he was "up to the nose hairs" in debt. He explained that the moneylenders granted him 1000 Glimolas in credit, and he was using every bit of it. In fact, he reckoned his needs to be closer to 1,250 Glimolas, only they wouldn't lend it to him. For the supplement he was "slow paying" his creditors, stretching his cash out thin as parchment. The whole conversation made me nervous. Then he told me what would happen if he couldn't pay the money back. "Well, if they go by the contract we signed," he drawled out in an exaggerated Eastern dwarf accent, "the moneylenders get everything I own, lock, stock and boomerang."

"What?" My voice was a high-pitched squeak.

"Well, we signed this contract." The accent made the words drop sleepily from his mouth. "Everyone does, you know. It's a contract where you have to put up collateral equal to at least twice the value of the loan. If you don't pay, they get to take your stuff." He paused for a long look up at the ceiling, as if the rest of his thoughts were somehow written on a dark rafter above his head. "Then, I guess, they sell your stuff to get their money back."

"Why, that's outrageous. Why would you sign something like that?" I was on my feet. We'd met in a tavern, a noisy one, thankfully, and there was a rowdy game of cards going on at the table behind us, so I didn't look too out of the ordinary. My face was flushed. There was an ache in my chest. "What were you thinking?" I pressed.

He just looked at me, opening yet another interminable pause. "I guess you don't understand. We all sign these contracts if we want to borrow money, everyone from the tiniest Dent to one of the Old Geeks. That's just the way it is. There are no options regarding collateral. Well, there is one. If you can come up with enough collateral in your business, you don't have to put your own personal stuff up too, but for most of us, that's a hard-to-reach 'if.' I'm just starting out, and all I have is in my business, so I had to put all of my stuff up as collateral, including my apartment."

Father smiled as I recounted this conversation and others that yielded essentially the same information about the mechanics of borrowing money. He shook his head and snippily said, "Whatever made you think a moneylender would loan you money for a good idea?"

I started into a speech about the value of good ideas, but Father just shook his head.

Returning to Mingus's cottage, the assignment completed, I started by apologizing.

"You made me mad. I thought you were teasing me about money. So mad that I didn't give you a chance to tell me the real story. I'm sorry."

"No need, young dwarf, this one was a particularly hard lesson, because it has to do with money, and money is not a neutral force in our lives. In fact, money is a very powerful and often volatile force. We treat it with special rules and behaviors that are specific to it alone, ones which rarely seem rational."

Mingus's health was improving. He was being encouraged to do some rehabilitation, so we bundled up for a walk around the perimeter of the meadow. The door slammed behind us with the help of a gust of wind, and we leaned into the wet air as we walked.

"I don't think we are quite done with money yet," he shouted over the wind. "What do you think you've learned about money so far?"

I went into my brain dump, recounting the interviews and correlating several of the Dent stories that had to do with money, especially with borrowing money. We did seven turns of the meadow, which made me sweat beneath my layers of clothing. My brain dump was beginning to repeat itself, and Mingus stopped me from starting through the same material again. We returned to the cottage and took up chairs on either side of the smoky fire. I added four large lumps of coal, releasing an explosion of sparks up the chimney. Settling into the deeply padded chair and looking into the fire, I felt spent, empty of information.

Mingus seemed to sense my energy drop and prodded me on. "What does all of this tell you?"

I started into the dump again. "No," he stopped me. "We both know the data, it's time for you to synthesize."

"I can't," I told him.

"All right, I'll start you out." He paused to clear his throat. "When you begin any enterprise you have to borrow money from somewhere. Whatever you borrow must be paid back plus interest. If you are not capable of paying the money back or if you otherwise break the agreement you have to surrender the collateral. The more you borrow, the higher the risk, the less you borrow, the less leverage you have. Are you with me?"

"Yes, I think so." Now that I knew he wasn't going to make fun of me it was easier to order my thoughts. I sat up straighter in the chair and continued. "The collateral is at risk for as long as you are operating on borrowed money." He nodded but didn't speak, waiting for me to continue. "So these profits we earn in our businesses, these are what must be used to pay off the debt, or at least reduce it if we so choose. Which reminds me, I talked to one Dent who had no debt. He had paid it all off, and was sitting on a pile of Glimolas, his own Glimolas—how nice that must be. Why would someone not want to be out of debt?"

Mingus turned his head and offered a half smile. "Some borrow money to grow a business," he said, "and then there are those who want to take money out of the business and are willing to remain at risk." He jutted his jaw out, sniffed, and added, "Each Dent seems to have a different tolerance for risk. You know, in the dark ages a person who couldn't pay a debt went to prison until payment was made, which for some meant forever—

life-everlasting! These are different times though, thankfully."

As Mingus added the words *Bear Debt & Allocate Profit* to the parchment, he mused aloud. "Somehow one has to balance the weight of debt, the need for money, and the desire for the finer things in life."

I was numb, but I agreed. "So, what I'm hearing you say, Mingus, is that a Dent must bear debt and allocate profit carefully."

"Indeed, young dwarf, very carefully, as you will be finding out some day soon!"

The Mingus Parchment

- *Survive*
- *Make the Deals*
- *Create a Society*
- *Bear Debt & Allocate Profit*

17 ~ THE TUG OF MANY

Leaving the office and going straight to Mingus's cottage became an almost nightly ritual. I ate well there, as his disability food-allotment was generous and of very high quality. It included Forest delicacies that a young dwarf could hardly afford, and the beer quota was generous enough for a family of four. I would help him with meal preparation and do the clean up. He would tell me stories about the old days, his youth, and most interestingly, fables about the ancient times as told to him by elders long ago. There was no particular pattern to the stories, but after several weeks of a smattering from one legend and a tidbit from another, I realized how little I knew about the days preceding the Great Glimmer.

Ours was a land of squabbling tribes under siege from several hostile non-dwarf neighbors. We bickered and fought among ourselves, then from time to time we were united by an external foe. According to Mingus, this uniting happened many times over thousands of years. It was a barbaric time in the Forest, yet many of the more pithy expressions passed down to us in the *Dwarf Book of Guidance* originated in this dark and violent era. It is sometimes referred to as prehistory because writing wasn't perfected until Glimmer's time. So what we know about prehistory was passed down in stories from generation to generation.

We finished dinner, cleaned up, and abandoned the kitchen for our regular cushioned chairs facing the fire. I prodded the coals, added two large hunks, dusted my hands, and settled back into my adopted chair. On the coffee table next to me were all of the transcripts from the Dent storytelling contest. The parchment sheets were wrinkled and dog-eared, like a deck of playing cards that had survived an ocean voyage in crews' quarters. I'd dealt, stacked, shuffled, and played with them almost every night since the party. Mingus, sitting in the other chair, reached for the white dragon, charged the old pipe and lit up. There had been a recent news item in the *Glimmer Globe* suggesting a connection between smoking and heart attacks. I was trying to convince Mingus to cut back. Much to my surprise, he'd agreed. This was his last of three pipes per day, which might not seem like a lot of cutting back to a nonsmoker, but to Mingus, whose pipe was always lit, it was a drastic and difficult change. Through the smoke, he continued a story he'd started while I was washing the dinner dishes. I'd lost track of it someplace along the way but tuned back in as he described the bloody invasion of the gryphons.

"Every couple of years (one gryphon cycle) the Gryphon Hoard would be sent out by their Great Mother Dragon, sent into our Forest to kill dwarfs for meat and rob us of our gold. Thousands of our ancestors were murdered in these campaigns, and mountains of dwarf gold were lost as well. These dog-sized dragons could smell gold from miles away, and each had a quota of a hundred freshly-killed dwarfs to stock the home larder for a full cycle. The whole Forest seemed helpless against the deadly invasions."

While he continued his tale, I mindlessly shuffled through the stories whose contents I knew by heart. I shuffled them into four stacks, rejoined them in a single stack, and shuffled them into separate stacks again. One time there might be three stacks, one time four, another time one. There wasn't any criteria really, it was just something to do with my hands while Mingus told his story.

"The arrival of the great dragon, a giant female, the mother of the entire gryphon hoard—the entry of that cursed monster into the mountains just north of the Forest—began a dark, bloody era, one which threatened the entire dwarf race. The Great Dragon was ten times the size of her offspring. Through some magic this monster gave birth to a slimy pod of fifty or so new gryphons each cycle. Because dwarfs at that time were so contrary—fractured into so many factions, fighting among factions and among themselves—they were easy prey. The villages closest to the gryphon lair routinely sustained the worst of it, and slowly this part of the Forest became a no-dwarf-land. Those who tried to stay were killed for sure. Those who moved deeper into the Forest and farther away from the mountains had a better (but not perfect) chance of escaping the gryphon hoard. After several more cycles, however, it became clear that the gryphons were relentless. They ranged farther and farther from the mountains, extending their hunting range until finally no place in the Forest was safe.

"Now you must understand that this was eons ago and dwarfs were very different than they are today. They were, in this ancient time, more like wild animals than civilized beings. They fought with each other and were, as far as we can tell, notoriously foul-tempered. There are several old cave paintings that suggest that gryphons routinely captured and killed dwarfs because the dwarfs wouldn't stop fighting with each other. As the gryphons harvested dwarfs and dwarfs fought among themselves, it seemed certain that dwarf nature itself was going to kill us all."

"Then the monks appeared." Mingus drew in smoke, exhaled, and paused as if he were remembering the scene from memory. "There was a group of holy dwarfs, monks, who somehow materialized in the midst of this otherwise wild, foul-tempered population. It was as if the few good dwarf qualities were somehow concentrated in this religious order. I say religious, but we have no idea of what their religion was about other than they were remarkably companionable with one another and, unlike the general population, demonstrated advanced forms of cooperative behavior. One thing we do know is that they were opposed to any form of violence between dwarfs, hence the walled monastery built ever so near the mountains. They moved into this no-dwarf-land, built a high-walled city with a single gate, planted the fields outside of the walls, and thrived. Cycle after cycle passed, thousands of dwarfs throughout the Forest were slaughtered and taken to the mountains as food stores for the dragons, yet the monks thrived unharmed, and the monastery grew as if it were protected by some sort of a spell. Even the most disagreeable of dwarfs became suspicious of how this city in the shadow of death managed to thrive within the hunting range of the deadly gryphons.

"After the worst gryphon rampage ever, six of the more powerful dwarf chieftains, dwarfs who couldn't otherwise agree on the color of grass, approached the monastery gates, intent on discovering the secret of the monks. At a banquet in the great hall of the monastery the Mistress Monk gave them their answer: 'Cooperate.' She pointed to the inscription above her head, high on the back wall of the great room. There it was, the one great word, and below it in smaller letters, 'The Tug of Many is Greater than the Sum of Ones.' The tribal chieftains, being contrary to the core, scoffed and berated the spiritual leader of the monastery and accused her of making an evil pact with the

Great Mother Dragon, exchanging dwarf lives for monk prosperity."

I had never heard this story and found myself wondering why, so I asked Mingus.

"This is an adult legend, one we keep from the young'uns because it is morally complicated and therefore reserved for mature dwarfs." He banged his pipe against the ashtray and absentmindedly reached for his pouch, caught himself, and setting the pipe down, grinned at me. Wringing his hands together as if to warm them, he continued. "The Mistress Monk was an elected leader. She was chosen because of an abundance of monk-like qualities: cooperation, patience, and caring being three of the most important. Confronted by this rabble of arguing chieftains, even the Mistress Monk had to use all of her powers to keep from losing her temper. She took a deep breath, gathered herself and after some minutes of silence said, 'Dwarfs, I will show you the power of cooperation.' She walked through to the far end of the hall and threw open seven great doors to reveal twenty-six gryphons. The gryphons meekly entered the room, approaching the monks like friendly dogs, nuzzling, panting, sitting, rolling over, gamboling, and whimpering. The chieftains panicked and rushed to the back of the hall, animated by fear and screaming for mercy, certain they were about to die."

I, too, was speechless and stopped shuffling the parchments. I sat up straighter and watched intently as Mingus sat back, relaxing his way into the best part of the story.

"The Mistress Monk explained that the monks had been attacked by the gryphons just as the other dwarfs had, only they devised traps to capture the beasts, then brought them back to the monastery where they were declawed and trained as pets. She explained that they were able to do this by cooperating with one another, and she felt pretty certain that if the dwarfs in the warring tribes could do some cooperating of their own they could defeat not only the gryphons but the Great Mother Dragon as well.

"As the legend goes, it took some time for the Forest dwarfs to overcome the habits of bickering and discord, but faced by yet another cycle of death they finally mobilized as one force. With help from the monks, the dwarfs trapped all of the attacking gryphons and domesticated them. Without food or family, the Great Mother Dragon left the hills and was never seen again. This legend is the basis for one of the more important sayings in *The Dwarf Book of Guidance*: The Tug of Many is Greater than the Sum of Ones. In short, cooperative solutions outweigh other solutions, and dwarfs working together as a team can do much more than the sum of their individual efforts."

Of course, I thought. This explains why it is so hard to do anything with a group of dwarfs unused to working together. I then thought of the parchments on the table next to me and, without any sorting, saw a pattern. Each story represented a Dent, and all of the Dents suddenly seemed to separate into one of two groups: the autocratic Dents and the team-building Dents. The autocratic Dents told stories using "I" as the main character, stories in which they had the help of employees but seemed to keep all of the power to themselves. The team-building Dents told stories using "we" and seemed to have abilities much like Mistress Monk in the legend. Those in the latter category were by and large the biggest companies, and the Dents in that group were the calmest and most easygoing, even though they said almost nothing about power and control.

I told Mingus about my notion and asked him what he thought.

"Yes, I think you are right." I was warmed to hear his agreement. "You don't need to talk about power or control if you understand how to engender cooperation and a spirit of common good. For once I think my rambling has produced something of value to you! I think this pattern is one of the Dent experiences you seek. How shall we put it, I wonder?"

Mingus's acclamation fired me up, and I was intent on getting the rest of this right. It was tempting to just use the inscription from the monastery wall, but it was a long and somewhat hackneyed expression, so I stopped before I spouted it out and thought for some time.

Mingus seemed detached, as if he wasn't even trying to solve the riddle. I looked at him, then at the fireplace, then at the mouth of the fireplace, then at the coals, then at the orange-yellow glow from the heart of the hearth, feeling as if I was being pulled into that intense place. Then it just came to me.

"Why don't we just call it 'Spirit of the Common Good'?"

"Perfect," agreed Mingus, chuckling. "You are in danger of becoming a wise young dwarf if you are not careful." And he laughed.

The Mingus Parchment

- *Survive*

- *Make the Deals*

- *Create a Society*

- *Bear Debt & Allocate Profit*

- *Promote a Spirit of the Common Good*

18 ~ I CAN DO ANYTHING, WELL ALMOST

Little Glow, our winter holiday season, is both a blessing and a curse. I know, I shouldn't say that. Little Glow is a sacred family and community time. But this year I was especially feeling the curse, in part because work of most types is effectively suspended for the whole month. The entire Forest shuts down, giving way to one party after another.

A whole month is taken up with celebrating everything from the Great Glimmer's Birthday to giving thanks for last year's crop of honey, the grape harvest, the wheat and rye harvest, and finally, the root vegetable harvest. The most important celebration of all, right in the center of the winter holidays, is the Great Geekus Bash. We are, after all, an economically advanced people, and the Great Geekus Bash has become an eating, drinking, gift-giving, pub-crawling, house-hopping, restaurant-frequenting blowout.

The Great Geekus Bash is in fact hundreds of parties wrapped into a three-day swarm, all subsidized by the seventeen companies that make up the Old Geek. The event goes for three days and nights with an optional six-hour sleeping window each morning between two and eight. The hard-core festival celebrants eschew any sleep at all.

All of the Little Glow celebrations are rooted in legend, which prescribes the method of celebration. It is a time of intense family and social intercourse, a yearly reweaving of Forest society's fabric.

As you might expect, my project was at a standstill. All the sorting, stacking, mulling, reconsidering, parsing, masticating, shuffling and free-associating had wrung me out. My mind felt like a desert, empty of ideas. And yet, facing a whole month during which any activity remotely serious or work-like was prohibited made me anxious and frustrated. The month was going to be a complete bust.

I tried to cheer myself with the sentimental side to Little Glow, the focus on family and friends. During the year, I had added one very important friend to my life and rid myself of an onerous enemy: Mingus. He had become both a friend and a family member. Yet I began to wonder if this was to be our first and perhaps last winter holiday celebration together, for Mingus was not getting better. I saw to it that he walked, even when it was cold and snowing, and as far as I could tell he was restricting his smoking to three pipes a day. Yet he was coughing more, and to my eye, he was losing energy. Certainly, there were times when he perked up, but he acted more like an old dog rising to chase the stick one last time. So this year's Little Glow began with a bittersweet taste.

Mingus, for his part, seemed unaffected by my low mood, and suggested that I put the Dent project on hold until the celebrations were over.

"This happens just once a year, young dwarf, and it is a time for fun and reconnection. Go and enjoy yourself. We will reconvene our work when it's over." If it had been Mother talking she would have invoked a canon of quoted advice, but

Mingus stopped there. He wrung his hands, twisting out the desire to smoke, or at least wrestling with it, and smiled. I found myself wanting to ask, "What if you don't live until it's over?" But I didn't.

What I did do was insist that he participate in the holiday celebrations with me. We requisitioned a wagon and two ponies, and I committed to celebrate the winter holidays with family events as opposed to the circuit of young'un bashes that would have normally been my fare.

Surrendering to the inevitable, I put the Dent quest out of my head and concentrated on seeing as much family and having as much fun as I could—all with Mingus in tow. It was a relaxing blur. Each afternoon I would appear in the meadow to take Mingus out in the wagon for that evening's event. We heard music with friends, ate with near and very distant family members, watched children dance, and—three weeks into the season—even spent an evening with many of Mingus's former colleagues from Bassenwaith Connistar Pty, Ltd at the yearly company dinner. The party was admittedly a little uncomfortable, as Mingus had not been the most friendly of mates, but he attended the do and certainly turned heads with his newfound smile and laughter—that alone was worth the whole evening. As we pushed ourselves away from a large banquet table after a multi-course dinner, a senior executive dwarf took Mingus by the arm and greeted him warmly with a hug, a gesture reserved for very close relationships. Both old men looked at each other, faces flushed and grinning.

"Mingus, what a surprise. I'd heard about your heart attack. How are you, my old friend?"

"I'm in for at least twenty more Little Glow festivals, maybe more. And how are you, Mortimer? I don't think our paths have crossed in what, fifteen years or more? Yes, how are you?"

"Well, life is fine. Miranda passed three years ago—hard, that—but life does go on, and I'm fine. How are you recovering? And what are you doing with yourself?"

"Well, I'm doing a little project in an area most foreign to you big corporate types. I'm helping a friend research the life of Dents. It seems he has an interest in becoming one."

"Dents? My stars, Mingus, that's a little far afield for you, isn't it? I don't recall you having any interests outside of the great corporate shelter. What's provoked this?"

"Well, the heart attack for one. I'm done at Bassenwaith Connistar Pty, Ltd. Put to pasture—very pleasantly I might add, no complaints—but out to pasture nonetheless. And so I have time, and my young friend here has involved me in this most interesting of questions: How is it Dents start and grow businesses?"

Mingus turned to me and introduced his old university pal, Mortimer of Mumblebridge, now risen to the position of Penultimate Vice President. I was stunned that Mingus would know someone that far up in the towering organizational chart. It also crossed my mind that he had not particularly benefited from such a powerful relationship, because although he was a manager, he was thousands of leagues below his friend Mortimer. I greeted him with a smile and a handshake.

"So you're considering the Dent's life, are you?"

"Yes sir, just considering it." I was imagining Mortimer returning to his desk, looking up my name in the roll of employees and marking me for disloyalty.

"That's a wild place to do business, down there in the sub-Geekus strata. Although I hear there are plenty of opportunities for hard working Dent dwarfs! But really, what's there for you to learn? All you have to do is pick the right product or service and ride it to fame and fortune. There is certainly some luck involved, but heavens, it's all tied to the right product, I'm certain of it! My old friend Mingus was a good business student. He knows how important the product or service is. I hope he didn't forget to tell you this, young dwarf."

"No sir," I lied, hoping to escape the encounter without his remembering my name. "If you will pardon me though, my parents are at table fifteen, and they are expecting me to put in an appearance to meet Mother's colleagues. It was a pleasure to meet you, sir. Mingus, I'll catch up with you later."

Riding home after the party we passed through a peaceful universe of falling flakes, our ponies' hooves muffled by knee-deep snow even on the main trail. Mingus was telling me about being in school with Mortimer, one story after another, indirectly revealing as much about Mingus as about Mortimer. When we neared his cottage I asked him what Mortimer had meant about Dents only needing to find the right product or service.

"Yes, that was interesting, wasn't it?" said Mingus, snow sticking to his beard. "What did you make of it?"

We rode over the last rise. Several of the houses were lit up, making the whole meadow glow. All of the trees within sight were loaded with snow. It was spectacular, and for a moment I was transfixed as we drew closer to the cottage. I suspected that Mingus wasn't asking me this question merely to make conversation, but as was often the case recently when I was close to an important answer or discovery, I froze.

"Yes?" Mingus prodded.

"For some reason I know it's important, only I can't think why." That was lame. Mingus said nothing. I pulled the reigns, and we stopped at his front door.

"I want you to think harder, and before you leave, give me an answer." This was very un-Mingus-like. I looked at him, snow still catching on his beard. I was worried about his catching cold while I blundered around this puzzle.

Finally he asked, "What are you afraid of?"

"I'm afraid that what Mortimer said is true."

"Meaning?"

"Meaning that to be a Dent you need a product or service that makes sense, one that will sell in the market place."

"Yes, and?"

I swallowed hard. "And I don't have one."

"So?"

"So? Well, so I can't be a Dent, because I know it's true."

"Good, you have at least half of it right. It is true, and we must add 'identify products or services that sell' to the list."

"What good will that do, if I don't have one? And I don't."

"It's late, young dwarf, but while you are driving home, reflect on the Dent stories we collected and note how few of them had real products and services when they began. I think you will be encouraged. You see, most of the successful Dents discovered the right products and services when setting out to become Dents, not before. Good night, now, and happy Little Glow yet again!"

"Identify products or services that sell" was added to the list, but I felt only a little better.

The Mingus Parchment

- *Survive*
- *Make the Deals*
- *Create a Society*
- *Bear Debt & Allocate Profit*
- *Promote a Spirit of the Common Good*
- *Identify Products or Services that Sell*

19 ~ HIS UMPTEENTH BIRTHDAY

I didn't like to think of Mingus being old, but in our culture, birthdays are very big events. And since he was turning Umpteen right after Little Glow, a birthday party was, we all conspiratorially agreed, mandatory. We knew he would resist. Even in a culture where birthdays are important, Mingus was a contrarian to the core, so we decided not to ask or tell him about the party. Since his heart attack and my search for Dent-ness, Mingus had gone from being a mean-spirited curmudgeon to a beloved family member. Mingus had been a big company man all his life, and most of those big company types have nothing but disdain for Dents. Yet here he was, I thought, leading the way, clearing a path for me, knowing that I may never actually succeed at it. Who knows, perhaps after we discovered what Dents do I might decide to stay with my mother's company, or get more schooling and become a professor, or do any number of other things and never become a Dent. There was no doubt, though, that a birthday party was in order, and the only way to do it right was by plotting a surprise.

With winter in full blow, I made my way to Mingus's cottage, having arranged to work on our list for the evening. I greeted him as I had so many other evenings, talking about the Dent search and anything else that came to mind. Before preparing dinner, we started (as we often did) by looking over what we had done so far. The physical evidence of almost half a cycle's work consisted of our pile of collected stories and that one single sheet of parchment, its words inscribed in an old-fashioned calligraphy with twists and flourishes from two generations ago.

If I hadn't been bursting with the evening's surprise, I'd have been discouraged. It was almost a month since we had fallen upon "identify products and services that sell." I had no clue about my Dent product or service to sell, nor had I a clue how much longer this Dent trek would take.

"Good evening, Mingus," chorused the family and friends who'd sneaked in through the back door of the cottage. They didn't yell "Surprise!" because truth be known we didn't want to surprise Mingus to death.

There were twenty-some of us: Mother, Father, and numerous new Dent friends, all dressed in the bright, clashing colors we dwarfs are so fond of. We gathered around the smiling Mingus as if we were going to have a family portrait painted. Few artists would have all of the paints necessary to capture this happy rabble, and after a group hug the efficient whirl of party-making was set in motion. Gifts were stacked, beer and food was paraded to the sideboard. There was a wealth of meats, cheeses, relishes, horseradish, blue peppers, and one small dish of beans. In the center of the feast was a great birthday cake, crowned with lit candles. On top was the likeness of Mingus, painted in sugar on rippled honeybutter frosting. The image was smiling just like its subject, our Mingus, who was finally speechless.

After some eating and loosening up a dwarf shouted: "Mingus, Mingus, we've heard nothing from the birthday dwarf. It's unlike you to be speechless, so speak to us, Mingus, speak!"

Over by the food a chant started, "Speak, Mingus, speak! Speak, Mingus, speak!" louder and louder, faster and faster until everyone was chanting as loud and as fast as they could. In a sign of surrender the old dwarf, red-cheeked, raised his hands above his head, assenting and motioning for an end to the chorus. Even so, it took several minutes before the chant stopped and the room fell silent. He stood, glowing red, teeth bared in a smile that parted his gray beard across his full face, eyes crinkled in happy exertion. He coughed, as smokers often do before speaking, paused again, and began.

"Well, aren't I the fortunate one?" he growled happily. "This is quite a contrast to last year's birthday, I must tell you that. In fact it is quite a contrast to most of the birthdays of my adult life." The room filled with cheering and clapping which slowly quieted as he continued. "Of course, the difference is that I have become a member of this family. Adopted, if you will, because of a most remarkable young dwarf who allowed me to join in his dream." He looked over at me. "And I want to thank you, young dwarf, for the kindness, a kindness which brought us together." More cheering. "And," he said, regathering the silence, "I must ask you all for a very special present, one which only an old man dare ask. I must ask you to see that this young dwarf finishes the work, learns enough to try out a Dent's dream. I ask this just in case I don't make it all of the way. You see, it is taking a devilishly long time to figure out this problem, and there is no end in sight, at least not yet." The room was still.

Mother spoke in a quiet, but affirming, voice, "We promise." Heads nodded throughout the room, all eyes on Mingus. "But," she continued, approaching Mingus, taking his hand and searching out his eyes with hers, "we also expect you to be here when the job is done. In fact, I think we expect you to make every effort to see this through until it is done and well beyond."

"Yes!" and cheers and clapping and more cheers followed until Mingus quieted the party again.

"Very well, not that I was trying to depart this world before my time in any case, but your promise is matched by mine."

The eating and drinking became more serious, stories were told, songs were sung, and Mingus received a table full of presents: many books and some bright winter clothing. One Dent gave him a new pipe stand made of gnarlwood that matched his coffee table and hutch, with enough slots to hold seventeen pipes. Mingus gleefully produced pipes from all around the house and filled all but one slot with wood, clay, and ivory instruments, each one of them charred and well chewed. The great white dragon occupied the place of honor, right in the center of the stand. He then placed the full rack on a high shelf among his many books, saying to those around him that perhaps it was time to just look at these beauties as opposed to smoking them, what with so much more work yet to do.

Later that evening, with the party well on the other side of midnight and many of Mingus's new family members departed, we sat talking with five Dents about the project and, in particular, the frustration Mingus and I felt about our lack of progress. We were all hovered over the parchment. "Heck, that's more than I started with, why don't you just take what you know and go do something?"

"Like what?" I shot back.

"Doesn't matter, really, just go do something. All this sitting around cogitating about theories isn't really going to get you anywhere. You have go to do something. That's what Dents do, they do things!"

Mingus interrupted. "Perhaps you all could help our young

dwarf a little more directly." He pointed his stubby finger at the Dent to his left, an old dwarf who owned a lending house, and said, "Tell our young dwarf again what it is you do when you 'do stuff,' as our friend here has so succinctly put it."

"Well I loan money, earn interest, and collect the money back."

"Good," said Mingus, cutting his answer off and pointing his finger at the next Dent. "And what is it you do?"

And so the answers came from each of the remaining Dents around the table.

"I bake and sell bread."

"I mine silver."

"I import and sell winter clothing."

"I build cottages."

"Good, good," said Mingus, having successfully navigated the roll call.

"Now, what you Dents don't seem to understand is that our young dwarf here doesn't know how to do any of these things, not one of them."

"Well you just have to get out there and try," barked the baker. "That's how I got started, no parchment list to help me. Just flour, milk, water, yeast, sugar, butter, and an oven. That was it."

"Yes, but I think the young dwarf would like to know where you learned to bake, say, your first loaf of bread."

"Oh," said the baker, a little deflated. He pushed out his

already prominent lower lip. "Well, the first loaf of bread was terrible. Oh sure, I knew something about baking from my uncle, who was a baker, but in reality I only knew how to bake one type of bread. Many of those early loaves went for bird food because, I promise you, there was no way to sell them."

"And where did you learn how to lend money?" Mingus inquired, turning to the moneylender. "And by the way, where did you get the money to lend in the first place?"

"Well, my father was a moneylender, so I learned the trade from him. But you know—I was given very little. It was a loan. And my friend here is right—you have to go out and just try it, keep doing stuff until it works."

"Or doesn't work, and you're broke," I groaned.

"Yes, that's possible too, only I have a special way of keeping from going broke."

"Meaning what, exactly?" asked Mingus.

The moneylender ran his hand along the front of his sweater, pushing the wrinkles out, and looked uncomfortable. "Meaning, and this is rather personal, I must say, meaning that I have a secret, a way I go about my business that makes me successful."

"Secret?" I asked. "What secret? How did you learn it?" I blushed, knowing that my curiosity had pushed me way beyond the bounds of propriety. "Oh, uh, sorry."

"No, we're all family here…of sorts. My secret is that I know how to choose clients, how to keep them from getting too far into debt, and how to make them happy about working with my company."

"Don't all moneylenders do the same thing?"

"No, indeed. Many moneylenders say they give good service, many say they know their clients, but none of them do it like I do...you see, it's in the doing!"

Mingus put his hand on the moneylender's shoulder,. "So you would be lost without this secret?"

"Yes, indeed," the moneylender proudly announced.

"And how did you learn about this secret?" Mingus asked.

"By doing. Didn't you listen?"

And there it was. Find a trade you know something about, then go and do it as well as you can. Be aware that you must discover the secret to doing it well. Nowhere in any of the stories was this notion of a secret mentioned. Nowhere! "I wonder why none of you describe this secret when you tell your stories though?"

"Because it *is* a secret," laughed the baker. The others laughed with him, but by the time the party broke up that night we'd learned that these Dents had never before consciously identified their secret, as such, and spoken about what it meant to them. They saw their secret as being accumulated knowledge, something that couldn't be articulated and probably shouldn't be discussed. Some were even quietly superstitious about it. But the fact was, each of them had a secret, and as these were shared on that late winter night, the evening of Mingus's Umpteenth birthday, we all learned a lot.

The baker's secret? He made unusual breads, sold only fresh loaves, limited his business so that he wasn't overcommitted, and ran a very happy shop.

121

The silver miner's secret? She had a special process to extract silver from low-grade ore. She bought old silver mines for a pittance and squeezed silver from what others thought was a spent asset. She also ran a safe mine, something almost unheard of. This attracted the best miners in the Forest.

The importer's secret? She knew where fashion would be in the future and imported styles accordingly. She also restricted her activity to medium-priced goods, as she couldn't compete at either the high- or low-end of the price spectrum.

The cottage-builder's secret? Build them one at a time. Build each cottage as if you were going to live in it, and select your customers as carefully as you might select business partners.

Just before retiring, Mingus added another line to our parchment.

The Mingus Parchment

- *Survive*

- *Make the Deals*

- *Create a Society*

- *Bear Debt & Allocate Profit*

- *Promote a Spirit of the Common Good*

- *Identify Products or Services that Sell*

- *Find Your Secret*

20 ~ POP!

It was two days after what could have been our last snowfall of the year. Small green shoots were breaking through beneath still-bare but budding trees. After months of winter darkness, we were being teased into believing spring was near at hand. It was the weekend, and I was bound for our village to shop and run errands. What with working during the days and visiting and working with Mingus in the evenings, Saturday had become, of necessity, errand day—to some a chore, but to me a welcome distraction from my perplexing problem.

Saturday became the big market day as Glimmerland developed into a modern industrial dwarf society and adopted the five day work week. I floated along among the hundreds of shoppers moving from stall to stall in the open-air marketplace and the village proper. Yes, even in late winter there were goods for sale in open stalls: potatoes, yams, apples, sausages, trinkets of all kinds, breads, jams, butter, milk, honey—everything a dwarf could need except for fresh vegetables, which would not appear for months. Oh, there were herbs grown in glass boxes, but there was very little that was fresh. Making my way through the stalls, loading my canvas bag with provisions, I approached the root vegetable stand and began to select my week's ration of potatoes.

The roots were available all year because of root cellars. These were underground warehouses, usually caves, where the root and apple crops were laid out on open-air racks in the dark. Somehow—we hadn't quite figured out the science yet—these roots were preserved until spring, when new crops were planted and the seasonal fruits and vegetables become available. Standing next to an older woman as she squeezed one turnip after another, looking, I presumed, for that perfect firmness, I heard her mutter something that sounded like "atoes." In a good mood because it was Saturday, and wanting to be helpful, I directed her attention to the mound of potatoes on the other side of the row.

"No," she barked angrily, "*Tomatoes*. I think I might kill for fresh tomatoes!"

"Oh," I blushed, "Sorry, I misunderstood." Thinking perhaps she was bordering on the senile, or more likely way over the border, I tried to salvage my pride by explaining in a calm, solicitous voice. "There are no tomatoes this time of year because they can't grow without warmth. Our winters are too cold."

"I know that, you young fool," she cackled, dusting me back by swinging her purse and attracting the attention of those within earshot. "Nonetheless, I would pay almost anything for a fresh, juicy, slurpy, bright red, tingling-tart tomato. As for you, why don't you stop bothering old ladies and do something good for society!"

The closing circle of curious dwarfs rolled with laughter, enjoying the show. Several barked encouragement to the old lady. "Yeah, tell him what you think, old gal." "Hey, she knows her tomatoes, what's the matter with you, hard of hearing?" "Yeah, me too, old woman, I'd give my house for a basket of tomatoes!"

Well, this was all very funny for them, but I was embarrassed. I hadn't meant to upset the old lady, and here she was making me the brunt of the crowd's sharp humor and growing sarcasm. My cheeks burned, my legs longed to run, and my day was ruined. I left the root vegetable stand and decided that I would abstain from potatoes this week, gladly. I pushed through the circle of meddling dwarfs. They followed me, jeering and laughing and chanting "ToMAto, toMAto, toMAto, toMAto," as if their brains were stuck. I remember saying to myself, "I'll get you some tomatoes, you old gryphon. You can sit on them and keep them warm all winter long!"

My favorite day, spoiled! All of the good feelings I had for dwarfdom turned sour. My day off had become a carbuncle, a hot knob of anger and frustration. Halfheartedly, I gathered the bare minimum for a week's subsistence—cheese, bread, and beer, mostly—then harrumphed, heading out of town towards Transition Meadows. I was marching to the rhythm of "tomato, tomato, tomato," which circled through my head like a drunk's song at closing time. The only way to stop it was to shout out my curse, "I'll get you some tomatoes, you old gryphon." For several steps the chant stopped. Then, as I continued up the trail, "tomato, tomato, tomato," started up in my head again, so I squelched it with a louder incantation, "I'll get you some tomatoes, you old gryphon." That worked. There was a blissful silence for several minutes, and when the chant started up yet again I was ready and uncorked it.

"I'll get you some tomatoes, you old gryphon!" I screamed at the top of my lungs. In the ensuing silence I heard a lovely, melodic voice reply, "Why that would be wonderful, but you should be careful who you call an old gryphon."

Turning in the snow, I looked up into the shining eyes of a dwarf priestess, one of the holy ones. She was dressed in silken white and gold priestess robes. Red painted lips formed her words and puffed them at me. She carried a red staff, and the hood of her habit seemed to give off a warm glow. I was spooked and jumped.

"Oh no, priestess, no, please—it's not you, er, it's nothing. I was talking to another, er, heavens!" Flustered and sweating, I fell to one knee in the traditional sign of respect accorded these priestesses by believer and heathen alike. My knee dipped well into a puddle, and the cold water reached up my thigh. I flinched, eyes downward, awaiting her invitation to arise.

Finally she giggled. "Arise, young dwarf."

"Thank you, priestess," I said, looking up at her but keeping my head low.

"I was flying about in the Forest when your promise of tomatoes attracted my attention. I might even be willing to act like a gryphon for such a rare treat, and you seemed so positive!"

I admitted to her that I didn't really have any tomatoes, and told her the story of the old lady. She nodded, smiled, and at one point covered her mouth as I described the crowd hooting at me. "I'm sorry, young dwarf, it's just too funny! See what the lack of fresh fruits and vegetables can do to people late in the winter?"

"Yes," I agreed, "but I feel more like a victim than a comedian." In fact I felt wounded by the whole experience, and having to share it with a priestess didn't help any.

"Well, young dwarf, I owe you an apology. First of all, I apologize for being a nosy priestess. We aren't supposed to do this, just drop into the center of your lives…but the thought of a tomato, well, it was just too enticing. And you're cold and wet as a consequence, so I will make good on my apology by fixing that." She raised her right arm, pointed at my soaked pants, and suddenly I was warm and dry. "Now for the more interesting part," she continued, "I sense something that your anger may have covered up. I sense that if you really had some tomatoes today in the market place, you'd be a wealthy young dwarf. Perhaps that old lady has given you an unnoticed gift."

"I don't understand," I said. "Unnoticed how? What do you mean? There aren't any tomatoes this time of year."

"Hmmm," she brought one finger to her red pursed lips. "I think," she said after a lengthy pause, "I think unnoticed gift is all I can say about this. The rest is up to you, young dwarf." I took a step towards her in order to ask for more information. She smiled and said in a whisper, "Yes, that is all that should be said," and rose slowly into the air and drifted backwards up into the trees, disappearing among the branches.

I'd seen priestesses before, and although I'm not a religious dwarf *per se*, these beings always evoke in me a kind of reverence, something I can't fully explain. Of course, any being that can fly ought to command respect. But it goes beyond that. It's as if there's some sort of deep connection that makes me get quiet and pay attention whenever a priestess is nearby. So it wasn't surprising to find myself standing in the middle of the path, awed by this encounter. I remained still for a long time, minutes certainly, until a wisp of the chant worked its way back again, only this time it didn't grate. "Tomatoes, tomatoes, tomatoes." I chuckled and started walking, back along the path, chanting. "Tomatoes, tomatoes, tomatoes," step, step, step, "tomatoes, tomatoes, tomatoes," step, step, step, all the way home.

As I unpacked the groceries, pushing bottles of beer into the dark cooling pit, loading loaves of bread up high in a cupboard, and setting the cheese in a covered dish, I knew what was next, only I didn't have a clue how to make it happen.

I had to find tomatoes—in the wintertime. If I could do that I'd have a real business. "*Yes*," I said aloud, "a real business!"

Just then I heard a loud "pop" someplace right in front of me, in mid-air. I knew it was the reply of the glowing priestess.

Right then and there, with that "pop" of affirmation, I became a dwarf on a mission.

21 ~ GLORIOUS TOMATOES AND OTHER VESTIGES OF VISION

Tomatoes, tomatoes, tomatoes, that was it! "Tomatoes in *winter!*" I told Mingus, and he laughed out loud. Mother and Father both said the idea was brilliant, and several of the Dents I was able to contact almost shouted approval. "What a jewel," one yelled. "It's a natural winner, you'll make a mixtillion with that one idea alone!" I was swamped by compliments and genuine expressions of surprise and excitement, all triggered by the prospect of tomatoes in winter.

Yet after each outburst, following each exclamation, came the same baleful question: "Tomatoes in winter, wow, but how?"

And the truth was, I didn't have a clue. But I did have this dream of covered stalls right in the center of every marketplace in Glimmerland, each piled high with my tomatoes: red, ripe and plump. I could see them, smell them, taste them! I could even imagine customers lining up to pay the winter premium for my magnificent tomatoes. Children were singing in my dream, the sky over Glimmerland was steel blue, and the distant mountains were deeply blanketed with snow.

I dreamt the dream, I imagined it, I thought about it, and I ached for it, only I didn't know how to do it. But that didn't seem to matter.

"I don't think I've ever seen you so animated," said Mother. "You act like you've eaten some psychedelic plant or you've been put under a spell."

We were having dinner with my parents. Mingus was now a regular member of the family. In fact, my parents were trying to convince him to move in with them, since I'd left a spare room and his health was not improving. Mother said that it wasn't a matter of improvement, it was just a matter of his getting older, and a day would come when he would need even more care than a visiting nurse could provide. That thought gave me a chill. I needed Mingus to help me. We weren't done yet! But for now he seemed alert and happy, traveled easily in the wagon, and was intent on remaining independent.

"If you get away early enough you should be able to avoid the weekend traffic at the River Mead ferry. That's the main hurdle." My father, ever a practical and cautious man, wasn't concerned with tomatoes. He was more interested in the logistics of my getting out of Glimmerland on the way to Southland. His concern was that I take the right steps to make an orderly passage from our winter-bound part of the world to a place where winter never comes...the great province of Southland.

Southland: a region where dwarfs go sleeveless, where the sun shines every day, where the trees are wispy and tall, the wind is soft and warm, and tomatoes grow all year around. Thus, a trip to Southland, three days each way by wagon, afforded me a double opportunity: first, to learn something about tomatoes, and how they grow, and secondly, to investigate the possibility of transporting (importing) tomatoes from Southland to Glimmerland during winter.

"Yes, Father, I intend to leave while it's still dark. That will get me to the crossing by sunrise Friday morning. Nary a single weekend wagon is likely to be there before I am." This placated Father, and throughout the rest of the meal we finished compiling a longish list of questions about tomatoes. There were three broad types of inquiry. First, how does one grow tomatoes? Second, what is it about tomatoes I need to know so as to be able to ship them? Third, why hasn't this been done before?

I was using two weeks of saved vacation to make this trip and was bursting with excitement, hoping that this was the last big push to the end of my search. I was ready to begin life as a Dent.

Mingus wiped some sweet cream from his beard, chuckling. "Well, young dwarf, you get the right answers, and you'll be out of a job in no time." We all laughed. What a wonderful dream it was, being out on my own, a real Dent, piles of tomatoes all around and my name known throughout Glimmerland as the King of Tomatoes. This heady stuff made sleep almost impossible. My brain was ready for the trip, but my body craved some rest. As is most often the case, the head won. Oh well, young Dents can suck it up. What's a little sleep compared with pursuing my vision of tomatoes in winter?

Mine was the first wagon on the ferry across the Mead the next morning. I followed the track south through villages and mountain passes and finally, at the end of the second day on the road, arrived at the Glimmerland-Southland border. I was paying for my lack of sleep, and the road was rough. Holes as big as cauldrons had filled with muddy water that disguised the wheel-shattering rocks hidden beneath. Whole sections of the road were simply washed out, and there were several places where I had to disconnect the donkey from the wagon, guide her around the rubble, then rig a pulley system to winch the wagon over or around the obstruction. By the time I made it to the customs gate at Southland I thought I understood fully why tomatoes weren't imported from Southland—the losses would be astronomical, because, as we all know, tomatoes are a delicate fruit.

"Ho there, dwarf, come down from the wagon for mandatory inspection," the Southlander customs officer yelled. I wasn't three feet from him and wondered why he was shouting.

"Down, I said, dwarf, if you value your life!"

"I'm getting down, what's the yelling about?"

"Do I hear a note in your voice, young dwarf?"

"No! No. Only I don't know why you're yelling at me."

"That does it." He reached up, grabbed my collar, and threw me out of the wagon onto the ground. "Support at the gate, support at the gate," he yelled. This was followed by the sound of boots thumping as more guards came running. In an instant, there was a booted foot on my throat, and I was surrounded by guards holding spear points against my body. I was stunned into silence, afraid to breathe too deeply for fear that one of the spears would actually cut though my clothes and really hurt me. Someone shouted, "Search the wagon!" I lay there while my single suitcase was thrown open, and clothes tossed and felt and discarded. The donkey was braying and the men were grumbling, but there was nothing else in the wagon. The suitcase was it.

"What have you to say about these?" one of the guards shouted, holding my lists of tomato questions and menacing me with them. A spear point was pushed harder against my neck. "What are you trying to steal, tomatoes is it?"

"Steal? Tomatoes! No, ah, sir, no I just want to know about them."

"Well, now we know! Tomato theft is a very serious offense. No wonder you tried to resist being searched. Take him inside!"

Four hours later I was released. Even in the twisted logic of Southland's zealous tomato-protecting guards there existed no authority for arresting a dwarf for tomato theft based on the speculation that a list of questions about tomatoes might be tantamount to stealing them. In short, there was no crime. But it had been made amply clear to me that tomato theft was indeed a serious crime. You see Southland, a place of warmth and plenty, had made up its mind that there wasn't enough to go around, that the abundance of this land was reserved for this land. In Southland it was a capital offense to export tomatoes. And the rule applied not only to tomatoes, but to all agricultural products.

After my mugging at the Southland border, I almost turned around and went back home. I already had the answer to one of my questions. I knew why no one was importing tomatoes from Southland. (Unappealing guards plus an impossible trip over unreliable and dangerous roads.) But I still knew next to nothing about tomatoes. And strangely, the image of my thriving tomato stands in the villages of Glimmerland seemed as real as ever.

I was in for a surprise.

Upon entering a large Southland village called Goldenwood and making my way to the market place, I encountered some of the friendliest dwarfs I had ever met in my life. These Southlanders, in complete contrast to the guards, were merry, courteous, and remarkably forthcoming about tomatoes and anything else I was interested in discussing. I spent all that day and much of the night asking question after question and getting more information than I ever would have expected. Late that night, in an inn I had chosen for my stay, we were into our beer and the hundreds of types of tomatoes that are grown in Southland. I was telling one of my new friends about my treatment at the border.

"Well, yes," he said, "We take the 'No Exporting' rule pretty seriously around here. You've got to be careful with those border guard types. They enforce the rules aggressively. In fact, you should know that the border is the only place in Southland where a traveler has no civil rights. Crossing is a dicey proposition. The guards can be nasty if they suspect you of anything, anything at all."

"I've been investigating this idea of getting tomatoes, only I'm obviously looking in the wrong place. I'll not be getting them from here."

The Southlander wrinkled his tanned brow, then asked, "What makes you say that?"

"Well, this is the only place I know of where the weather is warm enough to grow tomatoes during the Glimmerland winter, and you have an absolute ban on the export of any fruits and vegetables. So like I said, I'm looking in the wrong place."

The dwarf ran his fingers through long, graying hair, then said, "Well you can make good weather with some wood and glass, you know, and you've obviously overlooked the matter of seed."

"The matter of seed?"

"Yes, the matter of seed. Seed is Southland's biggest export. That's why we don't allow the vegetables out. We want to sell the world our seeds. As for weather, well, a little glass and wood, and you can make a place with good weather. You know, a hot hut. Don't you have those in Glimmerland?"

"Hot huts? No, we have what we call hot frames. You know, small glass-covered frames for sprouting seeds, but a hot hut is something we haven't thought of."

There was much more to my visit—trips to tomato farms, tricks about growing tomatoes, and a protracted investigation into the best seeds for use in a hot hut (assuming that one could be made in Glimmerland). I finally made a seed purchase and spent four days looking at hot hut construction techniques, wondering how I would raise the capital to build this unproven structure back home. By the time I left, the dream was still alive. I made sure my paperwork was in order for the border guards, and headed home. The trip back was just as long and miserable as the trip out had been. But I was a dwarf with a vision.

I'll tell Mingus, I thought, with my new-found confidence. We'll add "Follow Your Vision" to the parchment.

The Mingus Parchment

- *Survive*
- *Make the Deals*
- *Create a Society*
- *Bear Debt & Allocate Profit*
- *Promote a Spirit of the Common Good*
- *Identify Products or Services that Sell*
- *Find Your Secret*
- *Follow Your Vision*

22 ~ A LARGER CANVAS

The first crop of HoT HuT tomatoes sold faster than bees fly in springtime and at a fine profit, enough to make a large payment against the cost of our Hot Hut facility (an enclosed winter growing building) and to open HoT HuT stands in four nearby villages. The second crop was even better—we were learning something about growing tomatoes indoors. We added HoT HuT stands in six more market places, bringing our stands to a total of ten, which made us a regional Glimmerland produce player. Mingus loaned me the money to build the indoor growing building, our giant HoT HuT, and to fund the first year's operations. We made him Chairman Emeritus and, as you would expect, he was a powerful leader.

We decided not to compete with the Glimmerland summer tomato farmers. We would use the short outdoor growing season to get ready for winter when we were the only supplier and prices were much higher. In order to supplement cash flow and maintain our market position, we kept the stands busy during the summer selling local produce under the HoT HuT label. Of the many lessons we learned in the first year, one of the biggest was the need for fanatical cleanliness throughout the whole tomato cycle. We soon discovered that the natural growing season in Glimmerland was only about a third of the HoT HuT growing season. Our time was twice as long as theirs. So we settled into a pattern of growing and selling tomatoes during the fall and wintertime, reserving the late spring and summer for building new locations, adding growing capacity, and improving our growing, harvesting and distribution methods.

On the wall in my office hung the old parchment Mingus and I had used as a guide for starting and running the company. Now framed in gold and protected by pane of glass, it read:

The Mingus Parchment

- *Survive*

- *Make the Deals*

- *Create a Society*

- *Bear Debt & Allocate Profit*

- *Promote a Spirit of the Common Good*

- *Identify Products or Services that Sell*

- *Find Your Secret*

- *Follow Your Vision*

Each line echoed mountains of experience. All through start-up and our early success, this simple list proved itself over and over.

Survival. I thought about it every day. The hardest part about being a Dent was being solely responsible for the survival of the company—me, the Dent, alone.

Deals. I had to see that we made the right deals, and I made or influenced the most important ones myself. I negotiated for the locations of our new stands and promoted the HoT HuT brand throughout Glimmerland. I helped set the hiring policies for all HoT Huttites (our associates) and reported faithfully to my board of directors and shareholders (Mingus, Mother, and Father). I saw that our seeds were of the best quality, reviewed the purchase of wagons and donkeys for our distribution, and led planning sessions about our future expansion. All of these deals were my responsibility, but I got lots of help from my HoT HuT management team.

Society. We had decided that it should be fun to work at HoT HuT, and that every associate was part of our story. We had parties and lots of celebrations. We wore multi-colored outfits; formal business dress was not acceptable. We shared our profits, worked by consensus, and loved our work. New associates were hired by the team members with whom they would be working, and fun and energy were considered among the most important attributes they should have. We all believed you can teach people technical skills, but that (except for Mingus) people's attitudes don't change, so why not start with good ones (attitudes, I mean)?

Bear Debt & Allocate Profit. We (the shareholders and I) decided on a limit to our debt. We would remain internally financed for the foreseeable future. This meant we would grow at a pace that would build market share but not increase the risk of having a moneylender as one of our partners. I was given a generous salary, enough for me to build a house of my own and to save for my next life, after HoT HuT, though I must admit I couldn't imagine wanting a life other than this one.

Promote a Spirit of the Common Good. I was the Dent, and only the Dent. All of the work within HoT HuT was done by my management team and those who worked in teams beneath them. After the initial start up, my first priority (as suggested by

Mingus) was to find people to do the work *in* the business, while I learned about working *on* the business. This was very hard, because as soon as I got good at a task, I had to learn to let it go. In the long run, however, this was the only path that would allow HoT HuT to grow. My mantra became "I am the Dent, and they do all the work." I praised them for this, and we shared in the company's financial success together.

Products and Services that Sell. Tomatoes in winter turned out to be a winner. Soon HoT HuT, I thought, would also have peppers in winter, cucumbers in winter, and perhaps, some day, peaches in winter. Our biggest issue was the idea of an indoor growing facility—anyone could make one—so we needed to stay ahead of the copycats by gaining and maintaining dominant market share as quickly as our capital and resources would allow.

The Secret. We could grow tomatoes in winter and sell them in local market places. We were cheerful, and sold them in a festive atmosphere at a price that granted us a premium. And people gladly paid for this luxury.

Vision. I still remember imagining a colorful map of Glimmerland: a bright watercolor affair showing all of the villages and interconnecting roadways, mountains, and paths. In the center of each village was a tomato stand, my tomato stand. That vision pulled me along the terrible trail to Southland, helped me withstand the assault by the border guards, struggle with the reality that there were no vegetable exports allowed out of Southland, and to hang in there until the answer appeared— seeds and a hot hut. That vision grew to include regional growing centers stacked to the sky all through winter with vegetables and fruits of all kinds, and perhaps even exporting to lands farther to the north where the weather is even worse than in Glimmerland. I smiled each time I thought of this, and I thought

of it a lot because I knew it was an important part about being a
Dent.

23 ~ THE LAST CHAPTER

As Mother is fond of saying; "Keep your eye on the meatball," and for me the Mingus Parchment *is* the meatball. So it's not unusual to find me musing over the list. I was doing just that on a bright spring morning when a messenger arrived with the news that Mingus had fallen and hit his head.

"He's in the village hospital. I'm afraid there's a real worry about whether he'll wake up again."

I ran from my office, hitched up a wagon, and drove to the hospital as fast as my donkey would go.

I was yelling at the donkey to go faster, lashing out with the whip. Even so, by the time I arrived at the hospital, there were dozens of wagons parked out front. I jumped down into the mud, tethered the sweating donkey, whispered an apology in her long brown ear, and ran into the hospital entry hall. There were dwarfs everywhere, extended family members, many of the Dents who had been to our parties, the storytellers, and even the woman who had been in charge of roll taking and absentees at Bassenwaith Connistar Pty, Ltd.

"I'm here to make sure he is treated well by the hospital and to see if there is anything we at the company can do for him," this woman said. A remarkably nice corporate gesture, I thought.

Mother walked over and hugged me. "He's unconscious, and we can't tell much more. Seems that he just slipped and fell, hitting his head on the stone floor in his kitchen. Just that." Her blue eyes filled with tears.

"What about his heart?"

"No sign of a heart attack, but without being able to talk to him, well, it's hard to tell."

"Then he'll be okay once he wakes up?"

Mother wiped her eyes with a yellow handkerchief, touched her lips with it, as if thinking, then said, "I'm afraid the doctors are talking more like…if he wakes up, not when."

More tears. I lost sight of Mother's face. I flushed with sadness and anger, clenching my fists. "He has got to wake up!"

"He's old, my dear. We all hope he'll wake up, but he is getting old. He'll die some day, and we should be prepared for the fact that this may be his time."

"No! I have to see him, he can't die yet!"

Mother, Father, and I were led to his room. We were his family, or at least the closest part, and we numbly followed a nurse down a long corridor to the Head Injury part of the hospital. Mingus was in a large bed under a bright yellow down comforter. His head was bandaged and propped up on blue pillows. His eyes were closed and incredibly wrinkled. He was breathing in shallow spurts, little puffs in and out, his chest barely moving. His beard had been combed, his hands folded across his stomach, fingernails still dirty—from gardening, I supposed.

I went to him, laid both my hands over his, and just sobbed and sobbed. I wanted to tell him how much I loved him, but couldn't get the sounds beyond my chest. The moment words began to form, I sobbed harder. And although he was breathing, he showed no sign of waking up, no matter how hard I cried.

Hours passed. Mother took charge, and we decided to team up so as to be with him around the clock. I took the first shift, staying through the night.

Four days passed. The doctors tried to convince us that we should be encouraged by the fact that he was holding his own and that this state of unconsciousness was his way of recuperating from a severe trauma. I was completely unconvinced. I even prayed, many times.

The fifth day I was standing vigil with four of the original storytellers, including Ethring of Eton. We were talking about our times with Mingus, reliving the great storytelling contest. We reminisced about Mingus's discovery of Dent experiences, Mingus and his almost supernatural change from an angry product of large corporate life to a wise and vital dwarf, Mingus who was newly loved by so many.

Ethring, who had watched his father die in the River Mead, was a comforting spirit.

"Yes," Ethring began, "life is curly, even though this part of the curl isn't much fun. But look, he's still with us, and we have this chance to be with him."

"I know," I said, "but it still hurts so much to see him like this, to not be able to talk to him—I mean talk so he can hear me. I'm not ready to let him go!"

Ethring nodded, lips pursed. "We don't get to choose the

terms of our leaving, I'm afraid. But I'm not unsympathetic. I certainly know how you feel."

"I know you do, I'm sorry. I don't mean to sound so self-absorbed."

"Then don't be so self-absorbed, young dwarf." I was still watching Ethring's mouth, but his lips hadn't moved. I looked around the circle of Dents, confused. Above Mingus's head, in the air, a light shone, and it grew larger and larger as it moved along the wall to the far corner and settled with a "pop." The priestess was standing, hands at her sides, all in white except for her red lips and red staff and ice-blue eyes.

"I said don't be so self-absorbed, young dwarf."

"Priestess!"

"You're not helping him. In fact your self-absorption is slowing down his recovery."

"But it hurts me so much, I can't lose him!"

"Indeed, but there is an important lesson in what Master Ethring has told you."

"Yes?" I was too exhausted by the vigil to even argue.

"If you can live with this part of life, accepting that there is a greater scheme at work here, Mingus just might have more time left with you. But you must accept your lack of control. The greater scheme is controlling this, not you, not even in the slightest."

With that she disappeared with another "pop." I whirled around, looking at each of the Dents, one after the other, my eyes scanning Ethring last.

None of them had seen her. They were all just carrying on, talking quietly as if no priestess has appeared at all. I took a deep breath, about to shout out my experience when something stopped me, something that felt a lot like Mingus, or at least his spirit. I exhaled, sat down, and wept, and as tears flowed from my eyes to my hands I released my imagined hold on Mingus. I let go of him, crying even harder. I finally said out loud, "Mingus, if you must go, may the Gods go with you, and thank you for all that you have done." Just then I heard a barely audible "pop" and felt Ethring's hand on my back, comforting me.

The next day Mingus woke up. Word spread, and soon there were thirty of us jammed into the room surrounding his bed. The doctors were talking about real recovery, and although we were exhausted from the five-day vigil, Mingus seemed rested and full of good humor.

Ethring was talking. "Mingus, while we thought you were dying, we reviewed our time together and decided that perhaps your biggest legacy is the list of Dent experiences, the parchment that bears your name. You are the first person to make sense out of a seemingly nonsensical but very necessary phenomenon, that of Dents acting like Dents by starting and growing businesses. Now that you have rejoined us for awhile, I for one would like to see you take credit for the work. Why don't you consider teaching about your findings, helping prospective and beginning Dents learn about these truths? You could do a great deal of good in the world."

"It's kind of you to say so, Ethring," Mingus whispered. "Only I'm afraid there was a serious omission in our work."

"No," I interrupted, "we went over that a million times. We are done with the list, everyone agreed!"

"Yes, I know, and until my accident, I would have agreed

with you. But as surely as I almost died here in this bed, something very important is missing from our list. I'm a little surprised that one of you life-long Dents didn't see it—you, Ethring, in particular!"

"And what is it we've missed, Mingus?" Ethring asked, half smiling as he looked directly at the slightly older Mingus.

"Well, I think I will give you veteran Dents another chance, let you figure out what's missing. To do this we should start with what we know already. Somebody get some paper and we'll write out the list as it exists, only leave some space at the top and the bottom and don't number any of the items."

I had written this list so often I could have said the words backwards in my sleep. And to tell the truth I was a little annoyed. Mingus, always pushing! On the other hand, I was so happy to hear his voice and to have him back that I took paper and pen and, without any protest, wrote the list exactly as he requested.

The Mingus Parchment

- *Survive*

- *Make the Deals*

- *Create a Society*

- *Bear Debt & Allocate Profit*

- *Promote a Spirit of the Common Good*

- *Identify Products or Services that Sell*

- *Find Your Secret*

- *Follow Your Vision*

"So Ethring, do you—or any of you—see something missing?"

"No."

Mingus then pointed a questioning finger to each of the Dents in the room.

"No."

"No."

"Not me."

"Nope."

"I don't."

"Beats me."

Heads shook, there was some mumbling and grunting, all echoing the same sense of unknowing.

Mingus propped himself up in the bed while Mother punched the pillows down behind his back. He cleared his throat. He'd not smoked a pipe in close to a year, but his system was still recovering. "Let me add this to your thinking, then. Why is it you all are here today?"

"Because we wish you well, Mingus!" a Dent shouted, sounding a little angry.

"Yes, and thank you for that. It feels good to be wished well by so many people. But why were many of you here before I woke up?"

"Because we wished you well then, too, Mingus," said Ethring, who was now tapping his foot and squinting hard at

Mingus.

"Thank you again, but when I was sleeping—if I understand the doctors correctly—you did not know I was getting well. In fact, most of you thought I was about to die. So given that, why were you here?"

"Good Gods, Mingus!" I shouted "We wanted to be with you, even if you were going to die. I can't stand this!"

Mother looked at me, shaking her head as if to say, "That's enough, young dwarf." I was a little startled by my own shouting, so I shut up.

"You were all with me because you were willing to help me from life into death, would that be a fair statement?"

"Yes," said Ethring. My mother also nodded agreement.

"And?" prompted Mingus.

"Death is a part of life," said Mother.

"Yes," agreed Mingus.

And then there was a long silence. Mingus, Mother, me, Ethring, and the gathered Dents. Each of us was looking to the other for the next thing to say. Some mouths opened as if to utter an answer, but the room remained silent except for breathing, the humming of hospital machinery, the footsteps of someone walking purposefully down the hallway, the ding of a distant bell, and then a "pop."

"Life," I said.

"Pardon?" asked Ethring.

"Life, we have forgotten *life!*"

"But we are describing what Dents must do, not some sort of metaphysical laundry list for business dwarfs!" protested a blustering and frustrated Dent in the back.

Ethring broke in. "No, this list does not describe what Dents must do. It describes the experiences that Dents must master to succeed. That is what makes Mingus's work so original, and there is no life on that list."

A smile appeared on Mother's face, growing to a grin and, finally, full fluted laughter. "Of course," she said, "Dents must live a life. That's what this whole experience is all about. It's all about living life!"

"Indeed..." And Mingus turned pink and nodded his approval.

In ten minutes' time we had all agreed on the final wording of what has become known throughout Glimmerland as the Mingus Parchment:

The Mingus Parchment

- *Survive*
- *Make the Deals*
- *Create a Society*
- *Bear Debt & Allocate Profit*
- *Promote a Spirit of the Common Good*
- *Identify Products or Services that Sell*
- *Find Your Secret*
- *Follow your Vision*
- *Live Your Life*

EPILOGUE

I am writing this long after Mingus and Ethring have passed on. Mother is about to retire from Bassenwaith Connistar Pty, Ltd and is running for village council under several slogans, one of which is: "Dwarfs and their money should never be parted!" All of those years constrained by the large corporation have turned her into a bit of a radical. HoT HuT became a national player. It was a great run. We took the company public on the Forest Exchange, and I was eventually replaced by a younger president. It was time. My guiding star had been to bring the Mingus Parchment to life, pushing myself and Mingus's ideas as far as I could. We succeeded, and I remain grateful to him and all of the Dents who helped us conjure the list.

Mingus spent his last years as a professor at Dwarfish University, the first professor of Dentship. He taught hundreds and, by his own recounting, could not have had a happier life. I was not with him when he passed. He died in his sleep after a full day of lecturing and writing, the two things he loved doing most.

We did send him off with a great Passing Over party though. We gathered at the Drink and Tell, dozens of us, and told all of the old stories, many more than I have time to recount here. His ashes were kept in a red and white clay jug sealed with beeswax dyed blue. The jug, adorned with ribbons, was set high on a wooden stand in the center of the room so that everything we said could be absorbed by the ashes. We shared all sides of Mingus. He helped so many people! We also shared the stories about his less-endearing qualities, because we miss all of him, not just the friendly part. We relived the struggle to get the list of experiences figured out, and marveled at how life truly is curly. Early in the morning, when the stories were done and we had eaten and drunk to his life, we took the red and white jug and carried it in a long procession to a high ridge where he loved to walk in the spring and summertime. I scattered the ashes in the wind, and we wished him a safe journey. It was then, at that precise moment, that I understood Mingus's final message. He had learned so much in life, yet none of it seemed to make him happy. Then he began to teach, first me and then others. It was teaching that made him come alive. Teaching, sharing what he knew, giving his knowledge and experience to others made him happy! As the gray cloud of ashes spread in the wind, I knew Mingus was a truly happy dwarf when he passed. He showed us that all the knowledge in the world won't make you happy. You have to give it away for that to happen. In fact, all of that knowledge is useless until it is shared with others. I keep the jug in my study. The ribbons are faded, but blue wax still clings to the rounded lip. I keep it as a reminder of him and as a talisman to prevent me from being too self-absorbed. (I still have that tendency). I also keep it to remind me to share what I know with others—as soon as I can and as often as I can.

When we went public, I had lived through more than twenty years HoT HuT. It was not all growth and happiness. A couple of times we almost lost the whole thing. There was a great winter storm that wiped out three of our HoT HuTs, and almost wiped us out with them. We were committed to selling an early tomato crop and had to scramble to repair the buildings and sell the first two crops that year at a huge loss to make amends for our late delivery. Then there was, several years later, a food scare. A local produce grower contaminated their vegetables by, of all things, using dwarf droppings for fertilizer! The *Glimmer Globe* got hold of it. Dwarfs everywhere were disgusted, and who can blame them? All of Glimmerland just stopped buying vegetables for months. We spent more money on public relations that year than we spent on seed and transportation combined. We finally came out of it by creating a system of public inspection for our production facilities, a system that was controlled by an independent public oversight group. But all of this took time, and as time passed, our assets were literally rotting on the vine. We suffered horrific losses. Had we been highly leveraged we would have gone under, no doubt about it.

So when the great drum sounded, signaling the end of the Forest Exchange's trading day, the day our shares were first offered to the market, I was ready to move on. Yes, of course I'd always dreamed of running a public company, but as I began to size up the expectations of a new board of directors and Forest Exchange regulations, the task of succession worked itself to the top of my daily to-do list. Within six months, I was handing the reigns over to a compromise successor (someone who fell about halfway between what I wanted for a successor and what the board was demanding). That was two years ago.

And this is the first big task of the next part of my life, telling you this story. I owe it to Mingus and all of the Dents, past and present. He was a truly a great dwarf, and those were remarkable times: a sort of dark ages when Dentness was so misunderstood, yet so necessary. I have owed this debt since his death and now am paying it off, word by word, as best I can.

Although I did my best to develop skills in all of the Dent

experiences, the item that seemed to mean the most to Mingus was the one I found the most elusive. I loved the job, but I still find it difficult to Live a Life. Part of my excuse is that I worked very, very hard, with long, demanding hours, and part of my excuse is that I loved what I did with HoT HuT. Although I had learned the other lessons well, at the end of his life Mingus still had to remind me about living.

By the time I gave up the presidency, truth be known, I wasn't having much fun anymore. The price of success had been awfully high, and the feelings of accomplishment were muted. Often I felt just plain lucky to have succeeded. Looking back, it is now clear to me that I could have tried just as hard and failed. It could have gone either way. As I look at the red and white clay pot that once held Mingus's ashes, I want to investigate life more fully. I want to try to discover whatever life I am supposed to live now. I have a hunch that if my health holds up, the very best is ahead of me—not as a Dent, but as an ex-Dent, a dwarf who has accomplished a lot and whose full time agenda is "living life."

I have not seen the priestess since that afternoon in Mingus's hospital room, but I find myself wondering why she bothered to come back. I still wouldn't call myself a religious dwarf, but I have become respectful of some greater scheme. I've had plenty of proof of it in my life, lots of experiences with the good faction as well as the faction I don't like. Most importantly, I've learned the need to accept the whole thing just as it comes. It's just one of the good things about getting older. Another is helping my son tie his shoes and my daughter read books in the dim light about faraway places she'd like to travel to.

It is early evening as I write these last lines. I can smell meatloaf for dinner and hear the children playing in a tree right next to our cottage. It is a warm still night in this part of Glimmerland, fireflies are appearing, the window over my desk is open, and the candle flame reaches straight up, not wavering or flickering a bit, it's that still. In my mind I hear Mother's voice again saying; "Keep your eye on the meatball, young dwarf." I smile and shake my head. What I didn't know before, but I know now, is that the real meatball is life, and the best way to keep your eye on the meatball is to contribute to others, whenever and wherever you get the chance. My contribution to you is this story and the hope that it gives you enjoyment, knowledge and courage. As for myself, it's time to put down this pen and gather my family. We are embarking on a new life adventure together. As you'd probably guess, Mother has already given us our marching orders, several times. "We need each other," says Mother. " Don't ever forget—we need each other."

THE END

ABOUT THE AUTHOR

Walt Sutton has almost always been an entrepreneur. Other than a two-year stint at the start of his career in corporate America, he has worked for himself for forty-three years. In his first career he started, owned, built and sold four different businesses. At age forty-eight, he sold the fourth business, and he and his wife Deborah retired to Sedona, Arizona to start their new life. It was a dream come true.

Three years into retirement—an odyssey that is the makings of another book for another time—something grabbed him and wouldn't let go. Call it a mid-life crisis, call it a turning point, call it whatever you like, but Walt became obsessed, hooked really, by a chorus of haunting existential questions. Where had he been? What had he done? Why did he do those things? And more than anything, what was the meaning of his life?

One thing he realized was that he wanted to teach, to write, to be of service. He realized he had retired because he was exhausted from running his businesses, not because he didn't like business, but because he was just spent, used up. The time off and much of his reading made him realize that he was still deeply curious about business, not his businesses, but other people and other people's business experiences. This was the real turning point.

He wrote *Leap of Strength*, a book about the CEO role. Following its publication in 2000, Walt began giving speeches and workshops for CEOs and entrepreneurs. He flew over a million miles and gave more than 1,200 speeches on six continents about the role of a CEO and what it is like to be an entrepreneur. Now retired (again) from speaking, he continues to write and maintains a CEO coaching practice, providing strategic advice and guidance.

At age 72, reflecting on both careers, Walt says that he loved his first career as a CEO business owner, but his second career as a teacher and writer has been by far the most rewarding. Of course he's quick to point out that there wouldn't have been a second career without the first. Such is life.

Today Walt and Deborah and their dog Maude live on a small farm on Whidbey Island in western Washington. Their three children and two grandchildren live nearby in Seattle.

CONNECT WITH WALT SUTTON

wsutton@mac.com

www.tellthestory.com